INTRODUCTIO

When I started to write this book, I knew that I wanted to share fresh, innovative and interesting approaches and thoughts on the subject of procurement. There are many articles published on social media that discuss current best practice; there is established literature on the subject and there are consultants' websites populated with well-founded research, so the challenge was there. I wondered if I would have sufficient material to contribute; the more I thought about the content and started to write, the more I found my fears were unfounded.

My audience is targeted—aimed at practitioners—and in particular my goal is to support the development and leadership capabilities of aspirant Chief Procurement Officers (CPOs) as well as current CPOs, especially those who are in organisations that do not recognise the value of procurement or where their value proposition may not resonate with senior leadership. I single out both these groups as they each possess the authority to drive and implement change, however, the book is open to all team members as a resource to influence change. Throughout the book, I share contemporary and leading thinking on how procurement can be granted high-profile status within an organisation. Thus, all topics take on a very practical flavour and provide working tools, methodologies, protocols and advice that can be readily implemented. It is a book by an experienced practitioner, for other practitioners.

You may be wondering what the motivation is for writing this book. In short, there are two reasons. First, the opportunity presented by isolation during the COVID-19 pandemic and the second and more important reason is a personal desire of mine to openly share my experience in this field with others. I am passionate about the subject, and I was fortunate to have worked in businesses that valued procurement and provided challenging work to all those in the field. A former colleague of mine—partly in jest, partly serious—suggested I write a book after he read a post of mine on LinkedIn and found value there. So, I took up the challenge.

Since the early 1990s, practising procurement in the business world has been immensely challenging. We have witnessed global growth, economic contractions, downturns and localised disruptions to name only a few. As I write this book, we are facing something none of us have ever dealt with before, namely major supply chain disruptions brought about by the global coronavirus pandemic. These major events test the adaptability of procurement practices and the agility of the teams that meet these challenges. In each of these cases speed and process rigour need to be applied to secure value, whether it be in supply assurance, recast supplier relationships or renegotiated commercial terms when responding to changed conditions. Market tools such as the traditional tender or Request for Proposal (RFP) do not lend themselves well to rapid outcomes, especially when the urgency of the situation may require a project turnaround timeframe of one week if business survival is of primary importance.

When I and others in the procurement field have met and worked through these challenges, it has provided the opportunity to redesign protocols, methodologies and work practices so that greater efficiencies resulted. Procurement can better respond to unplanned circumstances, which in turn helps build a better business. As the late Sir Winston Churchill said, *"Never waste a good crisis"*, and many of the improvements that have been developed in reaction to these events are what this book shares. They have been tested in practical application, have generated the intended results—namely securing desired commercial value—and more importantly placed procurement as a top-line business function. The real benefit though is that they make the work of procurement more interesting, more challenging and more rewarding.

Not all of my 42 years in the workforce were spent in procurement. Roughly half were spent in the accountancy field before an opportunity arose to move into a commercial role and then to lead a team in procurement. I have worked in five countries, and my time in procurement has taken me to six continents of the globe, dealing with multinational and small businesses, local communities and a wide range of industries. These different experiences have enabled my exposure to many different cultures; I have met and worked with many capable people, learnt a lot from them and cumulatively they have shaped my thinking on the development of excellence in procurement practice. My personal aim, therefore, is to share the benefit of these wide and different insights for the advantage of readers.

Another motivation for sharing my insights is recognition that what made procurement successful in the past will not guarantee success in the future.

Recent changes in the business landscape have increased reliance and demands that are placed on procurement, so expectations have changed. Globally, businesses have moved to flatter organisational models; leaders have less discretionary time available, new markets have opened and will continue to do so, and supply chains can face sudden disruptions. Procurement needs to respond to these challenges and change its operating model.

The purpose of this book is therefore threefold:

- It teaches good practice in procurement that lifts the function to a new level, challenging much conventional thinking and application

- It shares information, and provides tools and protocols that help with immediate deployment of new and improved practices in the workplace

- It develops those working in the field to rise to a new, higher level and assume greater accountabilities, provides career growth and allows individuals to make a large and lasting contribution to their organisation.

I do not cover procurement aspects of large capital projects as that warrants a separate book to recognise the many complexities and specialised expertise of the topic. I do, however, refer to capital sourcing in Chapter 6 (Sourcing), targeting lower-value capital spend. Similar comments can also be made on procurement technology, enterprise resource planning (ERP) system design and logistics. These are all very wide and specialised disciplines within the field of procurement, and all are essential to the smooth running of the business. Reference is made to all of them throughout the book, but well short of what experts would write.

That all said, what I have written will make procurement fun. It will assist those wanting to transform a transactional, low-impact function to a strategic one and lift those strategic functions to a higher level and with that, create personal growth and job satisfaction.

It is the role of a leader to ensure that their team members should feel motivated to come to work every day and undertake challenging tasks that promote personal advancement, broaden their experience base and enable career aspirations to be met. This book can provide some fresh thinking to help that growth.

Finally, whether it is just one or all of the ideas in this book that are applied to and help build a better business through the leverage of procurement, I will have succeeded.

Enjoy!

CHAPTER 1
Getting the Fundamentals Right

When building a house, you need a good foundation and better still, through design excellence you can ensure low ongoing maintenance costs and retain value through build and fittings quality. So, getting the framework right is the best place to start. Whether it is building a house, or in any project requiring a clean-sheet approach, invest in good design and quality, and the benefits will flow for a long time.

There is no difference when considering the optimal design of a procurement organisation. Get it right—put the structures in place, resource it with capable people, deploy the right measures, have access to protocols and good technology—and the foundations are there for success.

Procurement needs a framework in which to operate—one that allows the organisation to function efficiently, have the right measures in place, have access to key business resources and have all the requisite controls in place through good governance. To turn this around, if you have a framework where some key elements are missing, the team and the business can never reach their true potential as unnecessary risk can be introduced, business decisions may be suboptimal, or some essential step in the process may be overlooked, resulting in value leakage. All that in turn may lead to downgrading procurement in the eyes of senior leadership, as well as in the supply community. The following diagram is a model framework of the essential elements of a high-performing procurement team. As you will see, leadership sits right at the top, followed by having a capable team supported by essential tools, processes and protocols.

Procurement Framework

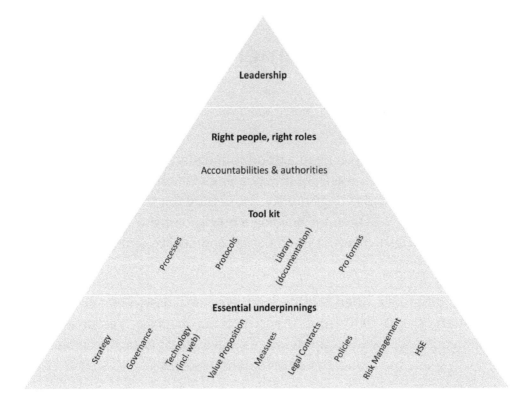

Of course, implementing all the elements in the framework is not an overnight task. It takes time, work, thought and care. Some elements can be developed quite quickly, but the essential aspect is to commit to the journey and implement it well.

The critical role and an essential prerequisite in procurement is that of good leadership. Its absence would be like an aircraft or a ship without a captain, a country without a prime minister. The concept sounds simple enough and easy to grasp, but what is often not considered is to recognise the level of work that the leader should operate. Procurement *is* a complex task—one that requires effective skill in communication, influence, technical aspects, commercial acumen, knowledge of the business and a leader must possess the drive, commitment and enthusiasm to succeed. The positive mindset of a leader will cascade into the team to lift their performance and thus assure business-wide recognition. The size and geography of the organisation, plus the magnitude of spend to prosecute will have an influence on size of the team.

As a minimum, the leader should be capable of developing and implementing strategy, working with and influencing boards and those at the Executive Committee (EXCO) level of a business to secure optimal commercial terms for its external spend base. If not in a peer capacity with those operating at an EXCO level, the CPO should be no less than one level below. If the CPO is too far down in the organisation, the authority to drive change is reduced, and accountabilities of the leader will be limited to the traditionally held view that the authority of procurement extends to price only and not to all cost drivers such as demand levers, service levels and specifications. The authorities of the role will thus be diminished and be constrained to a limited functional role. How the CPO can achieve this higher status and details of the work of the role are explained in the following sections and chapters.

The following are what the typical accountabilities of a CPO should look like to fulfil the expectations of senior leadership commensurate with a top-line organisational role:

- To design a requisite procurement organisation, resource it with capable people and to lead and develop members to reach their full potential

- To develop a procurement plan—for EXCO approval—outlining activities, projects, timeframes for completion and planned value, aligned and consistent with business annual plan objectives, targets and shareholders' expectations. To track and report performance of agreed key metrics on a monthly basis including forecast annual values. Counter actions for all negative variances against plan to be noted

- To ensure all protocols, measures, practices, and technology deployed for use in procurement are fit for purpose, are consistent with company policy and meet the needs of external stakeholders and the communities in which it operates

- To ensure relationship excellence with all internal stakeholders; including operations, finance, legal and others where there is mutual reliance for both procurement and the organisation to fulfil their business objectives

- To provide expert commercial advice when requested on any business matter.

Of course, these accountabilities can be flexed to meet, for example, a particular business direction undergoing major change, but the key requirement remains the same regardless of business context, namely leadership. The number of accountabilities should remain at four and no more than five, otherwise the role will be too big.

The authorities of the CPO (over and above vested authorities commensurate with level in the business such as financial and organisational) would include:

- To prioritise procurement plan activity consistent with meeting business plan objectives

- To negotiate and finalise commercial outcomes with external parties once approval for negotiation strategy is provided by EXCO

- To sign commercial contracts under delegated authority from EXCO

- To develop, implement and embed procurement policy within the business consistent with company values and profile.

So what of the CPO's team?

The overlying maxim is that it should be resourced with capable people and their work should be challenging and consistent with procurement's plan objectives. This is discussed further in Chapter 2 (Team Capability Profile), and a suggested layout for a procurement plan is contained in Chapter 4 (Procurement Steering Committee). The resourcing level of a team should be sufficient to prosecute the procurement plan.

For consideration, too, is the level of resourcing required to execute work outside of core procurement plan objectives of commercial value delivery (e.g., development of strategy, protocol development and technology considerations). All this is essential but should not be more than 15–20 per cent of those engaged in executing the plan. If the support group becomes too large, it can result in a loss of focus for the procurement team as other agendas and priorities can be introduced.

Each team member will have their own suite of accountabilities and authorities—depending on their level within the business, and consistent with the work required to be undertaken. The primary and overriding objective is to provide role clarity and with it a sense of challenge, stretch and consistency with procurement plan and business objectives.

Reverting to the framework above, and considering tools, processes and protocols, these are all critical lynchpins and—as they require more detailed discussion—they are explored further in the following chapters.

An oft-discussed topic is to whom should the CPO report. Should it be finance, operations, a leader of a shared services organisation or another group? I personally have worked in a number of different structures and the reporting line is largely irrelevant—any of these can work. What is important though, and does work, is the establishment of a Procurement Steering Committee (PSC) who is authorised to make commercial decisions on behalf of the business. The CPO would fulfil the role of secretariat, and the PSC should comprise of the Chief Executive Officer (CEO), the Chief Operating Officer (COO), the Chief Financial Officer (CFO), and others by invitation depending upon the subject matters of the committee's agenda.

I am passionate about this structure (viz., a PSC). It has the effect of placing procurement high in the organisation with the top-line leadership taking an active role. There may exist a functional reporting line for the CPO into a senior leadership position (outside of the CEO) but that is largely irrelevant as the real influence, direction and authority of procurement resides with the PSC and the senior leadership of the business. Members of this group will have authority to sign large-value contracts—it provides them with an opportunity to influence the desired commercial outcomes rather than performing an after-event review when the work has been completed. I discuss the PSC in Chapter 4 where I examine its role and mandate in more detail, including suggested agenda topics and typical documents for presentation.

Traditional business models place the procurement function as a service provider rather than one wholly integrated with the business and operations, with equal status. This is an important change from conventional thinking as the measures that can be applied to CPO performance will be those of the senior leadership team, namely bottom line financial performance, safety cash flow generation, working capital management and so forth. The degree of influence the CPO can have on these metrics can be significant. They may have further metrics specific to the role, such as supply chain assurance, but the key is to ensure that typical service level metrics such as *number of sourcing programs or contracts concluded, number of stock outages and number of contracts signed* are not the primary driver to guide priorities and performance. These are important but they are measures to apply to team members accountable for their individual spend categories.

Another topic that comes up frequently when discussing procurement organisation (and it is more relevant for larger businesses) is whether it should be a central group, a centre-led one with a distributed team or different teams operating independently from each other. There are definite merits in adopting a central model to leverage commonality where it makes sense such as for policies, ERP system design, standardised legal contracts, commercial deals for common suppliers, and goods.

My personal preference is to operate a small, centre-led function and to operate a distributed model—to allow procurement to be close to the business, its leadership and local priorities. In that way, it allows procurement to be integral to the business and its activities directly linked to business performance. The methodologies of working would all be the same—common protocols, common value policy and so forth—but the priorities of procurement, its plan, would all be operated locally. Reporting lines would be directed into the local business. The leader, of course, would have a relationship with the central group where the lead CPO would reside. All would share project activities through a common intranet, and in this way the synergies of the group can be leveraged across the business.

There is no fundamental reason why procurement cannot fulfil its rightful place high in the business or organisational structure, as in fact, it is no different to and is equal to stand-alone teams such as finance or marketing. The counter view, of course, is that procurement is seen as a group that does work on behalf of the business—it engages with the market and presents options and recommendations after negotiating the best possible outcome to their customers who either reject or accept the proposal. We should move away from this model for the following reasons:

- It places procurement in a subservient role to operations, namely with the right of veto over procurement's work and recommendations. Operations may select options which are suboptimal for the business as a whole but perhaps may be the most risk-averse to production

- It forces customer-centric measures on procurement such as *number of tenders/RFPs released, number of contracts signed, percent of spend prosecuted,* and *savings generated.* This drives particular behaviours and work priorities which in my view may be wholly incompatible with business direction. Instead, procurement should have essential measures applied such as *cash flow generated, costs eliminated from spend profile,* and other essential balance sheet and profit and loss metrics. This is discussed further in Chapter 11 (Measures)

- Given procurement's lower status within the business, it is denied a seat at the table, referring to business performance and strategy reviews. The influence that can be brought to bear by procurement as custodians of commercial strategy can be significant

- It diminishes procurement's negotiating authority in front of the counterparty when securing terms or finalising commercial positions. The reason for this is that the counterparty knows that no deal can be agreed to without reverting to the customer, thereby adding delays to the process

- Finally, it places procurement, through lack of business integration, one step away from the core business thus removing the function from day-to-day decision-making, priority setting and strategy development. Priorities can thus be set by others which may in turn compromise procurement's ability to deliver its full business potential from the best commercial options available.

Of course, the CPO's position at a high level in the business is one that has to be earned, not automatically granted. The CPO must be able to demonstrate that they are capable of fulfilling the accountabilities noted above and possess the requisite leadership skills. For those below the level of the CPO in the management structure and who aspire to fill the role, it is never too early to demonstrate leadership capabilities. This is commented on further in Chapter 18 (Conclusion). They will have the inherent advantage in that the profile of the work is very high and can attract top-level interest in the business given the impact the role has on spend, its profitability, business continuity and cash flow.

Continuing the theme of *Getting the Fundamentals Right,* you will see throughout this book an emphasis on simplicity. Thus, I steer away from bureaucratic, complex documentation and communicating through multiple layers of management. Instead, I focus on one-page documentation such as RFPs and other documents utilised in the sourcing process, getting to senior leadership quickly, and prioritising important and strategic information, rather than transactional. This is necessary because a well-functioning procurement team needs to be agile; if it is going to operate as a top-line function then the communication in content and focus needs to address the needs and priorities of top-line leadership. It is for this reason that we need to minimise bureaucracy and keep documentation short but powerful in content.

Before I leave this chapter, in summary, I advocate for the following:

- Strong, effective leadership and a team resourced by capable people

- Investing in the hard work of defining role accountabilities and authorities for team members and all elements of the *procurement framework* depicted above

- The establishment of a Procurement Steering Committee (PSC), with the right composition of organisational senior leadership

- Positioning procurement as a function that is fully integrated within the business, not as a service provider

- Keeping relevant documentation short, to the point and powerful in content.

Through my experience and what I have witnessed works best for procurement, following this list will ensure the fundamentals are correct going forward.

CHAPTER 2
Team Capability Profile

Given the magnitude of the challenge to introduce and operate a high-performing procurement function and the change management required to move from traditional models, the procurement team profile requires not only strong and effective leadership, but also requires members who have the collective requisite capability to deliver project outcomes aligned with senior leadership's expectations.

Thus, not only are technical skills, passion and commitment necessary for the work, but also, team members should have certain key leadership traits as mentioned in the previous chapter—namely have good business understanding, as well as communication and influencing skills across all levels.

Historically, many procurement teams have struggled to demonstrate their value proposition outside the only tangible metric of savings. Those organisations that measure procurement's source of value as *negotiated savings from original tender responses,* or using some other metric that is not hardwired to traceable bottom line impact, will continue to struggle.

Accordingly, new metrics of value need to be introduced, and these are discussed in Chapter 3 (Value Proposition and Value Policy) and Chapter 11 (Measures). In summary, a different balanced scorecard is required that shows the strategic response to the following:

- Managing risk

- Ensuring business continuity

- Savings that can be directly traced to the business bottom line

- New strategies to future-proof the organisation from major unplanned events.

This will challenge procurement in ways that have not been tested before.

Decision-making must be clinical and appreciate that in times of ambiguity, strategies must be agile, and priorities may shift on a weekly, if not daily basis. Team members must be capable of working in this environment.

Engrained approaches—such as *global category management*— which for many years have been the benchmark of success, are now being reconsidered. Value is being redefined and what worked well in the past, such as the classical *tender* or *volume leverage*, may have no role or little role to play in the future.

Relationship management has never been so important—both within the organisation such as between the EXCO and the PSC (which I discuss in Chapter 4), as well as externally with key supply chains. Effective reporting and influencing skills are essential to maintain executive support and avoid disruptions to the business and supply chains. Thus, procurement leaders and team members must recognise the importance of their role in the business.

It goes without saying the CPO must have the support of a capable team to deliver senior leadership's expectations, and the following are the minimum procurement team attributes required:

- Strong assertiveness skills through the ability to lead, shape and successfully conclude commercial negotiation activity. With that, an entrepreneurial flair so that creative options can be developed to overcome negotiation blockages or major sticking points

- Strong project management skills and an ability to work to tight deadlines

- Strong analytical skills (e.g., the ability to determine the true profit a supplier generates from a commercial transaction)

- Strong contract development and management skills

- Resilience

- Honesty, independence and trust must also be present, as team members need to operate free of influence or bias toward particular outcomes/suppliers.

The team may have accountabilities beyond the core work of sourcing. For example, there may be a need to have some team members focus on technology development, others who design and implement new digitised processes, an individual whose primary role is to look after reporting (e.g., into the PSC, extracting data from the organisation's spend profile analysis), and another may focus on strategy. As mentioned earlier, this aspect should be limited to 15–20 per cent of the total team size so that essential support-type work does not detract from the core objectives of essential value delivery—including supply chain assurance and essential contract management. Regardless of team size resourcing, the essential rule applies, namely, to have only capable people and those that can progress to assume other and greater accountabilities over time.

In summary, having the requisite team capability profile in place ensures that the team, through its leader, can meet the principal expectation set down by senior organisational leadership, namely, to deliver superior commercial results. With that, it will achieve high-profile status within the business, and as a capable resource, provide organisational capacity to undertake and manage more complex work—resulting in career growth and the potential for promotion opportunities.

CHAPTER 3
Value Proposition and Value Policy

An aspect I have witnessed in practice is how procurement can struggle to articulate their value proposition to the business. Further, if you were to ask individual team members what that proposition is, a different answer may result from each one. This is not a criticism, neither is it an uncommon occurrence; it confirms that procurement, when in the role of a service provider, is not a recognised top-line business function, unlike marketing which is relatively easy to define. That is, describing the service in a few words, and its value to the business and its priorities, can be difficult.

There are several reasons for this difficulty and they include:

- For many procurement teams, the primary source of value is price-based and includes *savings negotiated from original tender/RFP responses*. This is a mouthful and to many, it is what is expected of procurement team members

- Procurement teams often do not understand the business—particularly if the team is not integrated to the business—and that lack of understanding can manifest itself in suboptimal negotiated outcomes on key clauses in contracts, or uncertainty around when to revert to the customer for clarification and input; instead, decisions can be made which turn out to be costly for the business

- Procurement's drivers are at variance with the priorities of the business; their agenda and plans are incompatible

- Procurement is driven by too many rules; these place a straitjacket on process and outcomes.

Of the listed reasons, the first one is probably the most common. Two reasons drive this—the fact that there is no trace of measurable value to the bottom line of the business, and cost avoidance's impact on the business plan is not visible. They are merely "funny money" calculations that have no traceable business impact.

Of course, I am not suggesting all teams fit into this category. Much intangible value is appreciated through averting a supply chain crisis, improving supplier performance to meet expectations, as well as offering a safe pair of hands to execute a sourcing program. Trying to say all these things in one short, simple sentence can be difficult.

My proposition is simple and is bound up in the aspects articulated throughout this book including:

- Raising the level of procurement from a service provider to one wholly integrated into the business—thus measures of performance include those tightly integrated to the bottom line and are measurable to business performance

- The use of commercial award criteria (discussed in Chapter 5) which ensures a joint approach is taken with the business to ensure there is up-front alignment on how business will be awarded in commercial sourcing programs

- The establishment of a PSC which provides authority to procurement's agenda, its priorities and strategy

- A business–focussed value policy as shown below.

Perpetuating a *price only* authority in procurement will forever constrain its true value and thus the business, when it fails to introduce all the value drivers of total cost. In addition, the concept of a service provider also limits its full potential, as it places procurement as a lower-level function with limited authority.

I am passionate on this aspect and hence I offer the benefit of my experience of what works, particularly if procurement desires to be a top-level team in the organisational structure. I discuss the introduction of the PSC in the following chapter, but before that, there is one other essential element that underpins a high-performing procurement team, namely its value policy.

Following is an example of such a policy that forms the platform to drive procurement's value proposition, which will resonate and connect with senior leadership.

Value Policy;
Savings are based on run rate savings only, market movements, negotiated savings from RFPs are excluded

Measure TCI impact – not just price	Measure savings from an agreed baseline	Measure savings based on implemented initiatives	Exclude exogenous factors
• Savings are calculated on a Total Cost Impact (TCI) basis – i.e. including price, demand, specifications, other associated costs, process changes, working capital reduction, value enhancements and operational savings – on an annualised run rate basis (EBITDA impact) • Savings include recurrent savings as well as one-off cash benefits (e.g. inventory reduction, avoided capex, better payment terms) – these are calculated based on annualised impact using a 20% notional discount rate, i.e. for a working capital reduction of $1m, savings of $0.2m will be included)	• Savings are calculated against an agreed spend baseline (e.g. previous year actual spend) – not against Plan • Where savings are against new spend (i.e. no spend baseline from previous year), savings are calculated against current year's Plan • Savings value are calculated based on change in underlying value drivers that the initiative is targeting (e.g. lower contracted price from superior contracting and/or structural changes in supply chain, reduction in demand or change in specifications etc.) • Savings are calculated on the basis of total business impact	• As part of implementation for each initiative, detailed calculation of savings are calculated (with clearly articulated estimation approach where required) – and agreed by relevant stakeholder(s) • Achievement of savings are tracked by sites and Corporate procurement against targets in the annual procurement plan and reported to the PSC • Ultimate decision on whether or not to implement an initiative will rest with the PSC – any initiatives not implemented are not counted for savings	• No windfalls or penalties because of exogenous factors. e.g.: – Volume: For direct materials, account for changes in production volume – Prices: For commodity products (e.g. fuel), market rise and declines are excluded

In the example, you will see that all cost drivers are considered in determining how value is calculated and more importantly, market falls and rises are excluded as these are determined by market drivers which are outside the influence of procurement. This is quite different from what is found in most organisations—the real benefit is the direct and measurable impact that procurement has on the bottom line of the business. It is hence a very easy value proposition to articulate. It also resonates well with all senior leaders in the business and others, too, are clear on the purpose and role of procurement.

I commend its introduction.

CHAPTER 4
Procurement Steering Committee

The establishment of a properly resourced and tasked Procurement Steering Committee (PSC) is a critical cornerstone that underpins the success of any procurement team and can ensure it will be respected as a top-line function of the business.

To make it work and for it to be effective, there are a few core, critical aspects to get right in its design. These are detailed below, but before I get there and speaking from experience, establishing a PSC will not in itself drive procurement's success nor the elevation of its status within the business.

The ideal composition of the PSC should be the top leadership of the business (CEO, COO and CFO) as they are the ones empowered to approve major commercial contracts, have primary accountability for the profit and loss account and set business direction. The CPO will fulfil the role of secretariat. Those in top leadership want challenging work to do, as first and foremost in their minds will be questions like, *How can you help me improve my business?* or *What can you do to improve my business plan for the year?* or *What can you do to help improve the business's cash flow, reduce its working capital and/or reduce its cost base on a sustainable basis?*

There are of course other matters which are important to any business that may have a direct bearing on procurement. So, the agenda of the PSC must in part address this and it will serve minimal purpose by showing metrics such as *number of sourcing programs ran in the month, maverick spending, off contract spending* and many more related to governance and compliance issues. These measures are important, but they are within the authority of the CPO to monitor and respond to any variances from plan. One does not ask the CEO to get involved in such work.

Critical design aspects to consider:

- PSC resourcing; this is commented on above

- Meetings should be at least monthly, or more, depending upon business priorities such as business transformation or responding to a global pandemic such as COVID-19. Once specific programs end, then the frequency of meetings can be wound back to a monthly cadence

- Meeting agenda, including:

  - Executive summary, including highlights from last meeting

  - Both *rear view* (lagging) and *forward-looking* (leading) measures such as *value generated measured on a Total Cost Impact (TCI) basis* (see Chapter 11 on Measures for definition), *cash flow generated* in period as well as forecast values for the immediate period ahead and financial year

  - Procurement plan (activity) for the following month, highlighting major projects

  - Negotiation strategies for those coming up in the following month (see Chapter 9 on Negotiations) to be approved by the PSC

  - Approval of Best Alternative for a Negotiated Agreement (BATNA) positions that support negotiation strategies. This is discussed further in Chapter 9 (Negotiations)

  - Support and assistance required from the PSC to ensure successful sourcing programs (e.g., ensuring the path is cleared to execute a BATNA position with certain teams who may find difficulty in accepting the position)

  - As and when required, approval of procurement strategy and value policy

  - Other, including staff matters and lessons learnt from last meeting.

A suggested layout of a procurement plan is shown in the next section.

The impact of a PSC on the business can be powerful as it directly involves senior leadership in the large commercial programs. They are on hand to provide direction and expectations, clear internal organisational blockages, and confirm that the execution of the procurement plan is a business priority along with the quantum of value in the procurement plan. Further, it allows procurement to conclude commercial deals and projects within the authorised planned project values and timeframes without reverting to senior leaders for interim reporting and feedback. Leaders should be on hand to provide direction if there is material departure from the plan. This higher organisational profile provides a negotiation advantage with counterparties, as procurement will have the full support of the business to conclude project deals rapidly.

Procurement Plans—Design

Procurement activity should be structured into projects—including the development of new supply strategies, contract renegotiation work, sourcing programs, any midterm contractual reviews, and should have a forward granular view for the following six months. This would form a master plan and guide all procurement activity. Thus, a simple structure along the following lines:

Pro Forma PSC Report

Project	Leader	Start Date	Completion	Project Value	Cash Flow / TCI
XOX	AB	14/08	21/08	$ XX	TCI
PQR	CD	18/08	25/08	$ XX	TCI
ETC	EF	22/08	29/08	$ XX	Cash Flow

As you will see, the structure of the plan is a simple one but contains all the essential information to monitor and track progress. From it, data can be extracted to present in graphical format so that key highlights and aggregate data can be brought out for the attention of the PSC.

Report to PSC
CPO Report

Week X/52

Particulars		Comments/References	
A. Contracts and Supply Chain			
1. Contracts awarded in week X	6	New Contracts: 3 Renegotiated: 3	
Total Annual Contract Value	$20m	Process Compliant: 100%[2]	
2. Contracts under negotiation requiring PSC input	2	*Refer Att. 1 for commercial strategy for* **ABC** *Refer Att. 2 for commercial strategy for* **XYZ**	
3. Updated executive management summaries for category management strategies	X Y Z	*Att. 3* *Att. 4* *Att. 5*	*How macro factors are impacting the business*
4. Supply chain assurance: those supply chains at risk		**Sole source supply:** *Att. 6* **Financial stress:** *Att. 7* **Other:** *Att. 8*	

B. Financial	Week X	Forecast Q2
1. Negotiated savings from contracts awarded[3]	$	$
2. Cash generated (incl. price increase deferrals, price reduction, supply chain savings)	$	$

C. Decisions/Actions required by PSC	No.	Ref.
1. Negotiations strategies	2	*Att. 9*
2. BATNA approvals	2	*Att. 10*
3. Arising from category strategies	3	*Att. 11-13 (Oil, energy, int. rates)*
4. Arising from supply chain assurance	1	*Att. 14 stock pile y*
5. Resourcing	2	*Out of plan hire & supply chain management*

---

1. *Distribution: CEO, CFO, COO*
2. *Following competitive engagement process, duly approved by appropriate level of authority*
3. *TCI bases*

This critical management report contains all the relevant information of interest and importance to PSC members in running the business, as well as showing the impact procurement has on its financial performance. Further, necessary detail is appended so that PSC members are immediately taken to summary information and can refer to attachments, if required.

CHAPTER 5
Commercial Award Criteria

This in my opinion, is one of the more important chapters in the book. Had I applied what I describe below earlier in my procurement career, it would have made quite a material and positive difference to process outcomes, speed to contract conclusion, as well as simplifying negotiation processes.

Simply put, Commercial Award Criteria or CAC for short, is the basis under which business will be awarded to a supplier. It is a transparent, clear statement and lists the key requirements for a supplier to satisfy. All potential suppliers are treated equally as they all have the same set of award conditions to meet.

But it serves more. The CAC serves to:

- Build alignment between the business and operations, and procurement, for the essential conditions to award business

- It provides negotiating authority for procurement to conclude a deal without constant referral to the business and further, the business commits to the award criteria agnostic of supplier selection

- The criteria serve as negotiating anchors on business award and would appear in RFP/tender documentation. By putting in the right thinking here, the benefits will be:

    - Transparency to the supply community on critical information to focus on in their response. This will show we are easy to deal with, we are clear in our ask, and responses can be constructed against the elements of the CAC, making evaluation and comparison easy

    - It places us in control of negotiations as we set the parameters and it is up to the supply base to meet our needs and/or defend why they can't give us what we want. That then gives us the opportunity to challenge, push back or test their bluff, or accept if our expectations are not achievable

- By focussing on the important, we shorten timeframes

- Also, by focussing on the important—if we are successful in agreeing to those—it then helps us to a speedy contractual conclusion because the big commercial points are finalised and agreed upon, leaving minor clauses to trade

- It will take the supply community by surprise. They are used to the traditional evaluation parameters of *quality, service, innovation and price*, and now it shows the rules of engagement and basis of award have changed; we are serious in our asks and they know contract award will be done quickly, and on a sound commercial basis

- The CAC represents our ask—if we don't ask, we don't get; we need to be bold as we will only get one chance to get it right.

Typical elements of a CAC would include (This list is non-exhaustive and will require tailoring to each contract.):

- Service levels

- Legal contract compliance

- Health and safety

- Implementation risk absorption

- Alignment of commercial interests

    - $ - specific number, per cent reduction from previous year

    - Risk sharing

    - TCI requirement

    - Market demonstration of lowest competitive pricing

- Capabilities to perform the task (Curriculum Vitae [CV], capacity)

- Demonstrated experience of comparable work

- Logistics capabilities

- Climate risks and potential opportunities

- Speed to mobilisation

- Technology capabilities

The idea of course is not to make this a long laundry list of "nice to haves" or to turn it into a detailed service level request but should be 4 to 6 (maximum) points focussing on the key/the critical. Use a "horses for courses" approach. Below is some suggested wording to use under the headings listed above. The words are not locked in stone; they can be modified to suit but should not be softened, as no advantage accrues to the business.

Further, this is not be the place to list all essential supplier qualification and capability information (such as financial strength, safety programs in place, adherence to environmental standards, etc.). All that should be done through the business website where suppliers complete the *supplier qualification questionnaire* and furnish any supporting documentation required. In this way, procurement can focus on the important information.

For the record, I am conscious I bias my comments towards alignment with Operations' teams. That is a reflection of having worked predominately in the resources industry and it was with that group where I had most of my interactions. Of course, procurement needs to integrate also with sales and marketing teams so appropriate products are sourced to meet their strategic objectives (including product specifications and pricing models). Just on that I recall one CEO of a supplier company telling me, *"In my business, it is how well you buy that determines how much profit you make"*. Wise words. Therefore procurement has a critical role to play on business profitability both from cost and revenue perspectives.

The introduction paragraph to the CAC should be the same for all RFP/tender documentation, along the lines of:

Award will be based on the following essential criteria and suppliers should structure proposals aligned with these key elements. In addition, please ensure your proposal is supported by the leadership of your organisation; is fit for purpose for the supply in question, is aligned with the business transformation objectives of X business, and provide a clear demonstration of your capabilities:

- **Service levels**

  The ability to meet minimum specification/service level requirements provided in Attachment X. *(Note: It may be better to specify the application and what we need the goods for and what the service should achieve, rather than get locked into a straitjacket or too restrictive a specification, which may be a significant cost driver in itself.)*

  The ability to meet service levels provided in Attachment X; these represent current servicing needs and represent the maximum level required. Please structure your response on full-service level compliance, as well as on a proposed lite version, together with the commercial benefit that may accrue to the business (i.e., an alternative which may be technology introduction dependent and/or require some change management conditions) that meets the essential servicing requirements.

  The provision of a fit for purpose preventative maintenance program that assures the business that key assets will continue to operate continually throughout the contract period and can demonstrate flexibility to accommodate the business's growing and changing needs with new and replaced assets over the contract period.

- **Legal contract compliance**

  Compliance with our confidential information requirements:

  - Information generated or acquired as a result of this commercial agreement is to be treated as confidential by you, the *supplier*

  - You agree to sign a confidentiality clause that binds your management and staff

  Intellectual property developed during your engagement will belong to the business.

- **Health and safety**

  Evidence of a fully capable and documented health and safety system that is compliant with current legislation.

  Demonstrated application of your health and safety processes in the workplace that support an injury-free work environment.

- **Implementation risk absorption**

  Absorption of any implementation costs to support a seamless transition from the current service provider to new. *(Note: Here we could list the sort of costs envisaged under this heading [e.g., say in computing, software changes, training, hardware compatibility, docking station replacement, integration with existing fleet] so that a true TCI decision can be made comparing one proposal with another.)*

  Absorption of implementation risk to transition to new supply arrangement. Thus, no business disruption should transfer to the business as a result of supplier change.

- **Alignment of commercial interests**

  Alignment of commercial interests (including risk sharing arrangements that ensure appropriate incentives are placed on the supplier and the business to deliver outcomes consistent with essential service provision and the business operating environment). Our requirements also include:

  - We do not pay for any rework, failure to meet essential and agreed Key Performance Indicators (KPIs), cost of delays, and supplier staff training

  - A supplier capability that has strong project management skills, including the identification of your clear expectations of support from the business for you to be successful to meet cost, service level and timeline requirements

  - A response that differentiates the service provision between fixed and variable costs and that measured improvements introduced can be readily tracked through to financial statements of the business; thus, pricing transparency so that embedded improvements can translate to visible cost reduction

- As this is bundled service offering, the business requires to see the transparency of savings that can be brought through the supplier synergy of managing one contract rather than one or more of the unbundled contracts currently available for award.

Alignment of commercial interests, including risk sharing arrangements that ensure the project is completed successfully within time and on budget—the supplier will wear the risk of budget overruns, delays and failure to deliver requirements. Thus, we require a supplier with strong project management capability and the ability to identify your clear expectations of support from the business for you to be successful.

A proposal leading to a 40 per cent reduction in TCI to the business from 20XX spend of $X for ABC services within 12 months; this will be driven by technology introduction, continuous improvement methodologies, core pricing and a fit for purpose service level agreement, thus including price, demand, specification and service level drivers; in recognition of this, the business is open to consider an appropriate length of contract, a simplified commercial environment, and other criteria that the supplier may wish to propose.

A proposal that not only demonstrates the sharpest market-competitive offering today, but also with clear mechanisms on how pricing will be structured in each prospective three-month period to retain the ongoing competitiveness of the proposal.

A commercial proposal aligned with the business's transformational business objectives of a 30 per cent reduction in TCI for XYZ services from our current cost base of $X million. Attachment X provides an analysis of our current costs and further details can be provided on request.

A competitive proposal that aligns with the business's transformational objectives supported by transparency on proposed business's labour rates and key work programs that are required to meet minimum service levels provided in Attachment X. Thus, details such as an out-of-hours service requirement, as well as a competitive approach to out-of-service/out-of-scope requests.

- **Capabilities to perform the task (CVs, capacity)**

  The ability to provide a team of capable people to support the effective delivery of services, ready to initiate the assignment after contract award. Please provide CVs of those that will be assigned to this work that emphasise the compatibility of their skills (technical, people, project management and continuous improvement mindset).

  Demonstrated achievements as a supplier that emphasise the compatibility of your skills to complete the work envisaged under this RFP.

  Demonstrated ability to work with cross-functional teams and that through effective knowledge and skills transfer, and user training and coaching, a legacy remains to operate successfully without third party support.

- **Demonstrated experience of comparable work**

  Proven and demonstrated experience that you have the capabilities to manage all required services for a contract of this size and complexity.

  Demonstration of an embedded project management culture able to manage successful project delivery, within agreed timeframes and budgetary constraints.

  Demonstration of an embedded continuous improvement culture able to simplify core processes, eliminate costs and wastage, and transfer commercial benefits to the client on a sustained basis.

- **Logistics capabilities**

  Provision of a logistics strategy assuring the business that goods can be delivered in full and on time resulting in minimal investment in inventory working capital.

  A fully outsourced logistics strategy whereby the provider takes ownership of existing inventory and guarantees minimum requisite service levels for the business to function effectively.

- **Climate risks and potential opportunities**

  Demonstration of a zero-carbon footprint strategy in the production of XYZ and delivery to our operation.

  A strategy that can enable the business to reduce its carbon footprint to zero and enhance its environmental credentials with the community.

- **Speed to mobilisation**

  The ability to provide a team of capable people to support the effective delivery of services, ready to initiate the assignment after contract award.

  The ability to mobilise a team of capable people to client premises within two weeks from month X, 20XX, ready to initiate the assignment.

- **Technology capabilities**

  Proven technology platform/base to underpin requisite service levels, continuous improvement objectives, cost-reduction objectives through innovation, and support the business leadership in its core support to the local communities.

  An innovative technology proposal that aligns with the nature of our business, including cost-reduction objectives and the ability to provide core support to our local community customer base.

As mentioned above, the list is not exhaustive, and each contract will have their own unique set of criteria. Criteria, once developed, can be consolidated into a library and stored in the company's intranet, creating further efficiencies for procurement teams (see Chapter 16 on Technology). The effort put into developing these pro formas will pay dividends many times over as control over the supplier award process will firmly vest with the business.

The topic of CAC is picked up again in Chapter 9 (Negotiations).

CHAPTER 6
Sourcing

Sourcing is the "bread and butter" of all procurement teams and is the most common way by which contracts are formed and contractual relationships are established.

If the process is executed and managed well, it can provide lasting benefits and value to the business. In my experience, for every good sourcing program there is one that did not go as well as planned. Reasons for this may be driven by the time taken to conclude the project, the expectations of value falling short, the resourcing of the project at too low a level in the business, customer support unenthusiastic to support the final recommendation, or contract negotiations taking a long time due to difficulty in accepting minimum legal positions.

It may well be after honest reflection the percentage of *good* sourcing programs in some organisations may in fact be less than 50 per cent. The absolute number is irrelevant as anything less than 90 per cent would indicate process failings.

This is by no means a criticism of procurement teams. I liken it to a poor golf shot which could be due to a variety of factors such as the swing quality, poor compatibility of the clubs with the player, or swing defects that creep in over time, to name just three. In a sourcing sense, it could be a function of process, people, lack of requisite technology, or a host of factors. The critical aspect is to reflect on why processes do not run well and redesign them to eliminate root causes of problems.

This chapter is devoted to examining the many root causes of why many sourcing programs do not run well—and it proposes a radically new one that has been proven to work, results in superior business outcomes and develops strong customer alignment and sound supplier relationships.

Traditional Sourcing and Market Engagement

Consider the following example and reflect on whether this may be typical of business practice.

A contract is coming to an end and therefore the preparation phase begins to launch an open tender or RFP to the market. The justification of course for this action is that the business tests the market—all suppliers are provided with an equal chance to win the business and depending on the nature, size and complexity of the contract, it may be confined to local communities only. It is considered a fair process. In fact, it may resonate well with the company's procurement policies or stated values. Procurement engages with operations to ensure requirements are clarified—the legal team provides the latest supply contract to use and then the tender/RFP is launched. Three weeks is provided for responses, and after that passes, responses are collated, a period of response clarification is given and after which negotiations begin. After further time, it comes down to two suppliers—it then proceeds to legal contract discussions and finally a recommendation is made. Procurement claim value from the savings generated from initial opening supplier offers. Operations may or may not accept the recommendation depending upon the impact it has to their business due to cost challenges, safety aspects, if their preferred supplier did not win the business and other reasons. They may accept it, but instruct procurement to secure better pricing, thus extending the negotiation process. Finally, the process is concluded, a contract is signed and the business proceeds to contract implementation. The gestation period for the source program can last anything from three to six months, or longer, depending upon contract discussions or availability of key personnel in the business.

Diagrammatically, the process (or some variant thereof) can be described as follows:

Typical Sourcing Process

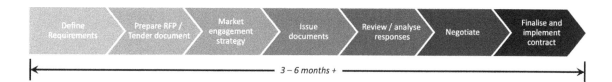

As can be seen, the process appears well-structured, but as described below, it is subject to numerous process failings which manifest themselves in time delays, costs and ultimately suboptimal commercial outcomes. The key weakness to the process is that it can take typically three to six months and possibly longer to conclude projects.

My contention is that documentation such as traditional open tender and RFP documentation may have outlived their usefulness as they have become long and complex. These and other failings are explained further below:

- Documentation is predictable with the supply community, thus weakening the buyer's position at outset

- The focus is on price and ignores other cost drivers such as demand levers (domain of operations), and stated service levels and specifications have limited flexibility and are areas outside the authority of procurement teams (confined to price only)

- There is no hard linkage to the business operating plan that ensures the business can meet its commitments to shareholders

- It places control with the supply community as they have the opening opportunity to provide a commercial offering which sets an anchor in the negotiation process. This may require substantial negotiating skill of the buyer to regain control at a later stage in the process causing cost and time delays

- Documentation often integrates supplier capability, safety and other requirements with commercial matters making the document more difficult to analyse and separate out important requirements with less critical ones

- It is more focussed on the *form* rather than on the *substance*; thus, RFPs as stated are long and complex, with an absence of CAC aligned with business priorities and objectives

- It is a document that supports a process, and not a strategic market engagement tool that places us in control of outcomes and thus the entire commercial negotiation process

- It is generally price driven and not structured on a TCI basis thus aligning with the negotiating authority of procurement rather than the total business

- It allows significant time from document release to supplier responses, thus detracting from the urgency in business decision-making. In business transformation or contract renegotiation programs, three weeks is too long a period.

So, the opportunity for procurement is that if we change the process, we can change the outcome; that is what the next section explains in more detail.

A New Process to Suit a New Environment

In order to overcome these process deficiencies and have one that is aligned with procurement excellence, a new process is required that is fit to support business programs requiring rapid results, is respectful of full market transparency and meets key governance requirements. This new process is shown below.

New Approach

The key difference in this approach is that great emphasis is placed on work at the front-end of the process and before any market engagement process is initiated. Once completed, teams are not only well informed and prepared, but they can also control the essential negotiation phase of work. In addition, they will have PSC approval to execute the task under fully delegated authority. A common expression in procurement, particularly in the negotiation phase, is *preparation is the key* and that is what this diagram shows. It allows the business to be in control through possession of key information on the market and its suppliers.

Questions Before Market Engagement

These questions need to be answered before market engagement (whether that be an RFP, a (re)negotiation, or an e-auction):

- Do we have a clear understanding of the market landscape and the number of suppliers who are interested in our business (and able to meet our CAC)? This may include sources such as emerging economies, particularly if there is product manufacturing involved

- Do we have a clearly defined CAC, signed off and in agreement with the business?

- Are we clear we will proceed to the negotiation phase with competitive tension (this includes a *sole source negotiation*), or in other words, do we have a strong BATNA? And, is the customer/business agnostic on supplier selection so that the best outcome for the business trumps existing relationships?

- Do we know if the quantum of profit the supplier is making from our business is reasonable? Are they a high- or low-cost producer? How important are we to them (will it seriously hurt them or are we a minor player?)? Do we know what the cost of a similar manufactured product from emerging economies would cost? Do we know what a good deal looks like?

- Do we have a clear fit for purpose specification/service level statement (not gold plated) and are we prepared to negotiate on that? This is important as often there is minimal leverage from a TCI perspective on price (e.g., labour rates) so we need to examine demand factors

- Do we know what our target savings on a TCI basis actually are for this particular product or project? Do we know the plan/budget for this item and last year's actual costs? What savings must we achieve? Is the business aligned on this? Do we know what the current spend base actually is, what the cost drivers are, and do we have an analysis of the current spend so we understand how these will change after sourcing?

- Are we clear on our project milestones, what must be completed when, by whom, and if deadlines are tight, are key senior players in the business available on deadline day to support business award?

- Do those in the business understand their role in this sourcing process?

- If we are proceeding to a (re)negotiation, has the strategy been developed, including a BATNA and a clear position on our competitive leverage?

- In summary, do we know what the potential savings are? Do we know how we will get them, the nature of the savings (price and/or demand factors) and when these will accrue to the business?

We also need to consider the following:

- An understanding of total business spend (volume and price) as well as current service levels, key specifications, number of suppliers, spend under contract, etc.

- An understanding of the business plan—what are the business requirements going forward, and what spend reduction is the business demanding?

- Use of price discovery tools—Request for Quotation (RFQ), Request for Information (RFI). These tools will give us feedback on what is possible and who out there is interested in our business. These are discussed further in Chapter 8 (RFIs and EOIs)

- Defining the CAC (*How will we award business?*) and presenting that to the PSC for sign off. One of the key requirements of any successful negotiation is to have a BATNA and the preparedness of the business to change suppliers to achieve commercial outcomes under acceptable risk criteria. What/who is the BATNA and this will need to be shared/ explained to key decision makers to gain their support. See Chapter 9 on Negotiations for a BATNA development worksheet

- Understand what constraints to value may be out there (change management, switching costs, risks) and to share these with the PSC for their consideration and guidance.

In summary, the objective of the planning phase of work—before any market engagement through sourcing—is to place the organisation in a position to award business on a sound commercial basis aligned with client's business condition. We can only do that if we are prepared, we have a clear strategy, a well-constructed CAC and a clear BATNA. We can then place ourselves in control of the process. It takes some effort, but the benefits far outweigh the work involved.

Whilst on the subject of understanding market dynamics, I should state that it is not unusual to rely on external market consultancies to provide this information and offer insights such as supply and demand characteristics into particular spend categories. I support their use; the challenge is to ensure the procurement team drives the consultancy to provide relevant and strategic market information that supports generating the right commercial framework for the future. Therefore, forward-looking and insightful information providing changed, or changing, market dynamics and other characteristics is highly relevant to procurement teams. My experience is that independent market consultancies do provide valuable information, but like all external service providers, they need to be well managed to add value to the business. Many tend to report on the past with little regard for future trends and market insights.

Before moving to consider typical RFP documentation, the work of sourcing may include contract renegotiation. In many respects this is a much simpler task, albeit the expectations of success in securing new commercial terms are very high. For that reason, the business needs a strong burning platform describing the urgency and reason for change or possess substantial marketplace data explaining why changes are necessary. The process described below is suitable for programs of business transformation or dealing with other crises (e.g., COVID-19) requiring supplier support.

A contract renegotiation would be structured to show the current business context, the reasons for approaching the supply community, its impact to the organisation and a request for help. Here the business can offer relaxation in specifications, service levels, contract terms, shortened payment terms in exchange for value transfer to the business. This process of supplier engagement can be a positive experience if it is structured along the lines of seeking true help and exchanging value on an equitable basis.

A matter worthy of raising at this juncture is the practice of writing to your supply base and asking for price cuts from previously negotiated contracts. This would typically happen when a business is under financial stress, say as in a COVID-19 world. The rationale is to reach out to vendors to share the pain the business is under, seek price and hence cost cuts for it to survive. If it does, the supply base also gains in that it too can continue to produce and supply goods.

This does not constitute a renegotiation and I do not prescribe to this practice. It is lazy and disrespectful. All it achieves is a disaffected supply base who will regard the business as a high-risk proposition and may well be reluctant to supply to the organisation in the future. The engagement with vendors in such a circumstance is not a positive one and can be quite stressful to both parties.

The preferred approach is as described above, namely, to engage the supply base and explain the business context with a pre-prepared script. The ask should be clear—as well as—and this is the important part—including what can be offered by the business to secure new, lower pricing. Aspects such as product range simplification, relaxation in service levels or specifications, simplified packaging, less onerous contract terms and shortened payment cycles should be considered.

I speak from experience; during the Global Financial Crisis (GFC) and during the current COVID-19 pandemic, the somewhat archaic practice of asking suppliers for price cuts was, and in fact still is, a common practice. During a business turnaround scenario a few years after the GFC in 2008/09, I was engaged in what is described above as the preferred approach. The outcomes were very different. Using the traditional method, I can recall success in achieving a level of price point savings, but if I were to be honest, the process of supplier engagement was not altogether a positive one, nor was the result an enduring one. In the case of the preferred method, significant and sustained savings were achieved through constructive engagement, relationships were positive as the supply base achieved benefits from the discussion and this endured throughout the contract term. Importantly, both parties benefited from the outcome.

It does take more work and more thought, but the outcomes are well worth the effort.

Contract Renegotiation

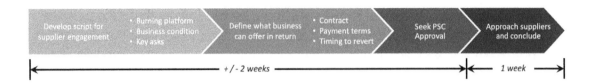

Structure of a Good Request for Proposal

A typical RFP (pro forma shown below) would be no more than one page simply stating the name of the business, requirements, how business will be awarded (CAC), when and who to contact. To simplify the process and limit documentation, reference can be made to the business website which contains the standard business contract, supplier qualification criteria and all submissions should comply with these requirements.

The structure of a good RFP should be:

- Crisp, short and to the point. We are clear on asks, we are transparent on our CAC, we advise when a decision will be made, how a decision will be made, and by whom

- Clear. It shows we are in control of the process, including negotiations, by providing clarity

- Aligned with what the business needs to achieve, not the market. Our requirements must meet this goal.

REQUEST FOR PROPOSAL
Supply of Goods and/or Materials

INTRODUCTION—Client context/burning platform

Our major focus and priority are to simplify all aspects of our business, remove substantial cost, and continue to operate safely.

REQUIREMENT

We are looking for proposals from capable suppliers who can supply the goods (as defined XYZ) to fulfil an annual requirement of XYZ for the purposes of *whatever the application is.*

COMMERCIAL AWARD CRITERIA

The award of business to the successful supplier will be based on the following essential criteria and supplier proposals should structure their responses aligned with these key elements:

- Minimum service level requirements including stock holding requirements, quantities, delivery times, etc.

- Minimum specification criteria *(Note: it may be better to specify the application and what we need the goods for/to do, rather than get locked into a straitjacket/too restrictive a specification)*

- Any technology/innovation requirements?

- Any key risks we want the supplier to absorb?

- A proposal leading to a X per cent reduction within 12 months in the Total Cost Impact to the business from previous year's spend of $X *(thus including price, demand, specification and service level drivers)*; in recognition of this, the business is open to consider an appropriate length of contract, a simplified commercial environment, and other criteria that the supplier may wish to propose.

NEXT STEPS

Proposals are requested by close of business on YXZ date; these will be evaluated the following day, including closing any queries the business may have. Potentially successful suppliers may be invited to present their proposals on XYZ date in person, telepresence or video conferencing technology). The client Executive Committee (EXCO) will meet on YYY, and make a final decision as to business award leading to contract signature by ZZZ.

(E-mail/telephone number) will be available throughout two consecutive days (*to specify*) and answer any queries you may have. No extension to the aforementioned dates will be possible.

This RFP is issued under client's RFP and tender terms and conditions, a copy of which is available at client website. (*indicate website address*). All respondents to this RFP will deem to have complied fully with its terms.

On the RFP, it is very important to link client's burning platform (equal to TCI of 10 per cent or whatever it may be) to the content of the CAC (refer to Chapter 5). The requirement will vary, but other elements remain—speed of process, alignment of business in developing CAC, preparation on determining what a *good deal* looks like, development of a BATNA, and the ability to change suppliers to meet the criteria. Business relationships with the supply community are key, but these get cemented *after* the deal and not during deal making, which is a common failing, especially with existing/known suppliers.

Again, this places procurement in control of the process—timelines, outcome requirements, and how and when we will make a decision.

One key aspect here is the surprise the supply community will get. They will need to focus on very short timelines compared to the past, they will have to issue short, focussed responses and it will really test their ability to align business expectations.

REQUEST FOR PROPOSAL
Supply of Consultancy Services

INTRODUCTION—Client context and why the need for services/ define expectations.

Our major focus and priority are to simplify all aspects of our business, remove substantial cost, and continue to operate safely.

Within this context, we seek proposals from capable suppliers for the supply of XYX.

REQUIREMENT

We are looking for proposals from capable suppliers who can assist/ support the business through its transformation journey to a low-cost sustainable organisation and meet the challenges of the current economic environment whilst maintaining service levels to our customers. We envisage a four- to six-month consultancy, working at our head office in location X, directly supporting XYZ and working with key members of the management team.

COMMERCIAL AWARD CRITERIA

The award of business to the successful supplier will be based on the following essential criteria and supplier proposals should structure their responses aligned with these key elements:

- Proven and demonstrated experience that you have done this work before

- The ability to mobilise a capable team of capable people to client premises within two weeks from XYZ date ready to initiate the assignment

- Demonstrated ability to work with cross-functional teams and that through effective knowledge and skills transfer, a legacy remains to sustain business improvement

- Alignment of commercial interests (including risk sharing arrangements).

NEXT STEPS

Proposals are requested by close of business on XYZ date (*say one week from RFP issue*), these will be evaluated the following day, including closing any queries the business may have. Potentially successful suppliers may be invited to present their proposals on XYZ date in person, telepresence or video conferencing technology). The client Executive Committee (EXCO) will meet on YYY date and make a final decision as to business award leading to contract signature by ZZZ.

(E-mail/telephone number) will be available throughout two key dates to answer any queries you may have. No extension to the aforementioned dates will be possible.

This RFP is issued under client's RFP and tender terms and conditions, a copy of which is available at client website (*indicate website address*). All respondents to this RFP will deem to have complied fully with its terms.

Through this approach, we have laid down the rules, we have made it very clear what we want, when we want it by, the format, how and when a decision will be made, and the fact that we will be making a decision quickly. Suppliers will like this.

It does mean though that we have to align the executive team through the PSC (or an EXCO team) to coordinate what is happening, to be available, to participate along the way if required, to establish the openness to make a decision on a defined suite of criteria (i.e., agnostic as to who gets the business) and that we are going to do this. It will mean that this will become the #1 priority in the business as all employees may be impacted (e.g., time, information demands). It supports a cultural change of our ability to make quick decisions based on facts/the essential and key commercial criteria/business impacts. Their input and influence into the design of the essential award criteria is a key requirement.

It also means we have done sufficient market research as to who to invite to the RFP process—the business cannot invite *everyone*—do we want tier one only, or tier two? Does our pre–reference checking/website review, or other work determined through an RFI/RFQ/price discovery, work to help us get to that RFP shortlist?

The CAC should comprise the key elements of what makes a good deal (usually structured around commercial aspects, service levels/specification, timing factors and capability requirements). Maybe some key-risk criteria may also be included, depending on what the service is, but it has to be enough to include the essential key aspects of the deal. Once this is agreed on, finalising a contract should be simplified as the key terms will have been satisfied. Developing CAC requires thought and working closely with the business.

One experience I can share is that after issuing an RFP requiring a turnaround timeframe from the supply community of four days, leading to contract signature after a further three days, a tier one supplier was excluded as they were unable to meet the required four-day turnaround of the proposal presentation. They were still focussed on developing proposals aligned with the *past* (viz. developing a PowerPoint deck of some 80 to 100 pages) and required more time. They failed to recognise that all that was required was the answer to the four aspects articulated in the CAC.

Short of labouring the matter, traditional RFP processes/documentation deployed by most businesses are incompatible with a business seeking cost reduction, regardless of magnitude, or whether the desired outcome is improved supplier capability or identifying the best supplier for the task involved. In fact, RFPs/tenders do very little to build a better business at any stage of an economic cycle. They are heavy instruments that are perceived to ensure a business has ensured market competition. They are overused tools that place control with the supply base as vendors prepare the opening response (market pricing) from which the business has to negotiate, and generate complexity, cost and very rarely, if ever, achieve business aims of internal cost reduction. This is because we measure cost impact on a TCI basis (this is explained further in Chapter 11 on Measures) which factors in prices, service levels, specifications and demand factors; an RFP structured under traditional practice is the sole and typical negotiating authority of procurement.

Much time is spent on training staff on the art and skill of negotiation, whereas this can be simplified and transferred to business at the outset if a well-structured CAC is developed. The organisation then sets the rules by which RFPs must be structured to align with business parameters.

I recall I was once asked to review an RFP that had been issued to the market and in addition to what I have listed previously, I offered commentary in the form of the critique outlined below. In fact, what I provide below is a clear example that *less is more*, proving that it is often easier to write and design complex documentation rather than write short, focussed ones. The long documentation merely adds time, cost and complexity into the process and fails to allow the respondent to provide relevant information in a prescribed format. Writing short documentation is a skill and does take time! Here is the commentary I provided:

- The amount of detail requested detracts from directing the supply community to focus on the main issues

- With all the rules we have laid down, the complexity of the specification and a lack of clarity in CAC, there is no impression we are commercially minded, we know what we want, we are a good business to deal with, we make fast decisions nor that we have done our homework well enough to demonstrate we know what we want and what a good outcome looks like

- What we have unwittingly done, is to ask for a huge amount of detail from the supplier in a vague form that creates complexity. The business has to analyse it, clarify it, negotiate it, all of which adds time and money into the process

- We ask for proposals to comply with *overall competitiveness and value*; this is very vague language. What does value mean?

- We seem to be focussed on complying with the process of completing an RFP rather than the outcome required by the business; this is evident in the very detailed specification document

- For the foregoing reasons, and our lack of preparedness, I would not have authorised its release in its current format.

The best way to lift the mindset from following traditional sourcing methodologies such as the classic open tender and RFP, is to *think of outcomes, not process*. Following strict processes can add significant delays and cost to business, not to mention the supply base. It can also lead to a disaffected supply base unwilling to participate in future programs and a demotivated procurement team.

Therefore, once consideration is given to a stricter prescription of what is to be achieved and the outcomes required in sourcing programs rather than how many boxes and sign-offs are required (as well as consideration to how many steps actually add value), much greater efficiencies can be introduced. For example, the end goal will ultimately result in leaders in the business signing off that a particular commercial outcome is acceptable or adds the most value. So, by having this group involved at the outset on key acceptance criteria (which can be translated into the CAC) and fed into the PSC for sign off, simplification naturally results, and speed to outcome can be achieved as well as improved commercial outcomes.

The key learning is that following process for process's sake is a non-value-adding activity and will rarely, if ever, achieve the desired commercial results. I recall earlier in my business career, the rule was, *As long as you follow process, we will protect you regardless of the outcome.* The question that needs to be asked is, *What happens if it is a flawed process or indeed does not result in a sound business decision?* You should not be afraid to ask "why" when confronted with or asked to follow a complex and lengthy process.

Whilst still on the topic of *sourcing*, a further comment to add on the need to follow open competitive processes with a minimum three quotes, is to consider what the financial threshold should be to undertake a market-competitive process. I have seen this set as low as A$5000. The rationale may well be to give *everyone a chance to win business* and the perception that the result will achieve the lowest price because of competition. These low thresholds may have some historical significance, meet a community expectation or exist for another reason. Apart from driving a lot of work and complexity into the business, there are alternative processes to follow that result in lowest total cost (not just price) and the best outcome for the business. These include:

- Sole source awards (always with a supporting, developed CAC) for those who have demonstrated their capabilities to the business in the past. This is a positive engagement process as it rewards good supplier performance

- Consider asking the local community to form an enterprise as a one stop shop for the business that covers representation of all local businesses. CACs for new commercial awards are developed and sent to them to consider who best to win the award

- Follow the essential elements of the new process described above but tighten timeframes to five days; issue the one-page RFP (with the CAC), allow three days for responses and award business on the fifth day. The risk is small and if an enterprise is keen to win an award, they will meet the deadlines and be incentivised to put their best offer forward at the outset.

Capital Procurement

As I mentioned in the introduction, I have not placed emphasis on procurement aspects relating to major capital expenditure (such as major plant, infrastructure and building development) but smaller items of capital expenditure that normally fall within the remit of procurement (items such as fixed plant or mobile equipment). Normal sourcing principles apply as described in this chapter and some suggested award criteria noted under Chapter 5 (Commercial Award Criteria), but other aspects which may take on greater significance in capital procurement would be:

- Payback considerations are an important measure, particularly when a business is facing cash flow difficulties. In these cases, a payback of two years or less should be sought. Net Present Value (NPV) is often used as a measure of value but that is not one to use in a cash-constrained environment as the underlying assumption with NPV is the business will be operating for many years

- Compatibility with existing equipment, as this may impact on spare parts inventory holding strategies

- Whether a redesign of business process can avoid the need to spend the capital

- Impact on the business's debt position (for capital-intensive industries this is a significant consideration [e.g., marine, aircraft, resources] as a high level of confidence has to be placed on future company revenue streams)

- Well-constructed acceptance criteria, including equipment commissioning

- Spare parts inventory and access to ongoing support, if required

- When comparing supplier responses, lowest price is just one consideration. Greater emphasis should be placed on evaluation methodologies such as net present cost analysis or life cycle costing, so that aspects such as equipment servicing, life of major parts, access to spares, future pricing of spare parts, performance warranties, guarantees, residual values and so forth are factored into comparison.

The list is not exhaustive, but it does indicate the need for strong operational support into the development of a well-constructed CAC.

To summarise and respecting there is a reasonable amount of detail in this chapter, the aim is to simultaneously simplify the sourcing process and improve commercial outcomes. Following the recommendations outlined in this chapter will achieve this aim and further, it will enhance the profile of procurement within the business and the community, save time and money and remove much bureaucracy from the organisation. The following is a summary of sourcing processes (typical and new) and brings together what has been said above:

External Spend Management

Typical Business Approach

- Heavy / exclusive reliance on process, use of RFPs/RFTs
- Default of competitive sourcing
- Work usually assigned to low levels within organisation
- Value determined as "negotiated price improvements from initial supplier responses"

- Documentation is long, complex, expensive and 'market predictable'
- Price focussed
- Supplier lead responses that set negotiating parameters
- One size fits all

- 'Process compliance' rather than Plan management / business outcomes
- Little work done prior to market engagement

- Risk averse, heavy reliance on specification compliance/retention of service levels
- Operations unwilling to assume risk for commercial reward

- Supplier relationship building rather than cost reduction

New Approach

- RFPs / Tenders have outlived their usefulness as a tool for supplier selection – the focus is on business bottom line impact after disregarding market price movements
- Total market opportunity/understanding
- Understanding of Plan costs, business drivers, and senior management expectations and assuring outcomes meet these requirements
- Business focus rather process focus

- Process light, emphasis on speed and value capture
- One page RFPs, RFQs, etc.
- Better use of RFIs (Request for Information) to determine if supplier base suitable
- TCI (Total Cost Impact) rather than price so that outcomes directly traceable to the P and L account

- Much work to be done to align business requirements, customer needs, flexibilities, min/max specifications, risk appetite and importantly, to align the executive team to ensure Plan requirements meet. This in turn provides the authority for Procurement to engage the market and close deals if cost reduction targets met
- A simplified process compliance environment, centred on front end controls

- Development of total cost reduction opportunity, decision making at senior levels; often plant technical specialists (traditionally risk averse) will stipulate their needs. Their input is respected but the contract decision (often based on $ levels) should be made by the CEO

- Challenge specifications/service levels – understand impact to costs of business. The focus is on the business, not on supplier continuity.

CHAPTER 7
Services Procurement

Services procurement can be a more difficult and complex aspect of sourcing, distinctly different from goods and materials, which may be easier to define and specify. What is included under this heading are several spend items including such expenditure as:

- Maintenance contracts

- IT support services

- Outsourced contractor work

- Legal and other professional services

- Large consultancies to support an Enterprise Resource Planning (ERP) system implementation or a business turnaround project

The list is far more extensive than this—too many to mention—and each one has its own unique differentiating factors due to various and sometimes quite specialised markets and particular business requirements.

A further complexity is that often, due to the specialised markets they serve or due to some unique skills possessed by a supplier, a sole source negotiation results. I belong to the camp that says that a sole source negotiation can be justified as long as value is received, it is subject to scrutiny by the PSC (depending upon contract value), and the risk of utilising a new supplier outweighs business benefits. In these cases, Chapter 9 (Negotiations), suggests a strategy on how to conduct a sole source negotiation.

All service type contracts have their common features, namely:

- Each will require a developed CAC—we need to be clear on the output that we want, when it is needed, the quality expected, and the skill level that needs to be applied. A suggested CAC for services procurement is included under Chapter 5 (Commercial Award Criteria)

- Each will require a *price*—whether determined by time and materials, fixed, a combination, or other. What is *fair* may be determined by competitor data, if open to the market or if not, previous work done, and a reasonableness test agreed to by procurement and the lead business customer

- It is usually essential that a senior business representative is seen as the *owner of* the source program/contract, as expert supervision may well be required and is often essential to ensure appropriate guidance is given, project management is applied and the output (or outcome) meets the quality expected

- Often, the involvement of legal support may be necessary, particularly if intellectual property aspects may have to be considered.

Speaking from my own experience and where I have devoted more of my time in this area, is on maintenance and external contractor spend. This is by far the more common type of services procurement; it is typically outsourced and, in most cases, would certainly constitute the larger portion of recurring spend.

Here are my suggested key elements to focus on when considering this category:

- Ensure the business gets the A-team; anything less may compromise quality, involve rework, or drive inefficiency

- Ensure all contractors are qualified with respect to skills required and, demonstrate alignment with the business from a safety perspective (i.e., demonstrate consistency of values expected, behaviours)

- The work is well scoped, acceptance criteria well defined

- The work is supervised by experienced, capable business personnel

- The work is planned well in advance, otherwise expensive costs of mobilisation may be incurred (e.g., equipment, people, air freight charges).

My experience demonstrates that if these elements are not apparent or well managed, it can add substantial costs to the business in rework, scope creep and above all in client dissatisfaction that can lead to disputes and potentially supplier community disharmony if sourced locally.

Too often I have witnessed procurement teams in this category focussing on *price,* namely, labour rates, and lowering it as their value driver. However, very often the single largest driver of cost are man-hours rather than labour rates, and by controlling those through good supervision, job planning and scoping, is where best value will be achieved.

Also, involvement from legal teams is essential in these types of contracts, particularly around aspects such as:

- Process to agree to scope changes or increases and impact on project completion and costs

- Payments; this may be important depending on contract length and ensuring the contractor's cash flow is not compromised. Consideration, too, should be applied to defining events as a suitable milestone for payment

- Hiring and firing contractors

- Risk allocation between contractor and business when considering aspects such as rework, time overruns as well as disputes generally

- Guarantees and warranties

- Project reporting.

Naturally, a "horses for courses" approach should be taken based on contract size and impact to business.

Further consideration may be given to a *bonus* in the event work is completed ahead of schedule. I favour consideration of this aspect as it keeps the contractor focussed and as a secondary benefit, the contractor would not accept the clause unless they knew there was certainty of scope of work, quality expected and there was a capable project representative from the customer/business. That in itself drives the right dynamic and behaviour. If a project is brought in ahead of schedule, the client benefits as project NPV will increase, as value will accrue to the business earlier, thus creating a "win" for both parties.

The hiring of external consultants to support large projects, like an ERP system implementation or a business turnaround, usually involves substantial financial commitment. Under Chapter 5 (Commercial Award Criteria), I suggest a typical CAC that may be utilised for such a spend item. The basis of engagement is essentially no different to that described for maintenance contracts, however, in this type of spend the demonstration of having done similar work before and with success, resourcing it with the best people and having some share in project risk (i.e., financial) are all essential minima. These contracts can be notorious for cost overruns and scope creep resulting in delays, client dissatisfaction and disputes. The right for the business to be part of the interview process—to ensure only the best people are selected—is also be essential, as is the right to fire or replace those personnel who are not suitable for the project. The business also needs to appoint an experienced and capable leader with appropriate role-vested authorities to manage the consultants and the related project to ensure key deliverables are met, manage costs and scope as well as deal with issues as they arise.

In summary, services procurement represents a more complex area of sourcing compared to goods and materials, however, the principles applied to this category are similar. The most critical aspects lie in the specification of what is required, ensuring appropriate skills are apparent and defining acceptance criteria. All of these require thought and input from operations as well as procurement. Experience would show for these reasons it can be an area of client dispute/dissatisfaction, but through good supervision of work and strong contract and relationship management these can be overcome.

CHAPTER 8
RFIs and EOIs

I have devoted a chapter to this subject as an adjunct to the previous chapters on sourcing and services procurement, as I believe these are highly underrated tools and that are not deployed much in practice. Their potential can be huge for market and price discovery information and, can lead to substantially shortened and simplified source programs. At the very least, their use will place the buyer in a well-informed position going into a source program, thus providing the buyer with an increased level of control in the negotiation and contract finalisation process.

These protocols can be quickly deployed in practice; responses can have a relatively short turnaround given the lack of legal commitment that flows from them, and they often focus on a few specific aspects of supplier capability making it easier for respondents to complete.

Request for Information (RFI) and Expression of Interest (EOI) documents also provide the opportunity for the business to explain to the supply base its strategic direction, key supplier capability requirements and thus prepare and test the supply base to see if there is alignment in business objectives and gauge a supplier's willingness to be a part of it.

Experience shows suppliers, for the most part, are willing to provide requested information as it represents an opportunity to showcase their business and demonstrate how they can provide supply solutions that meet requirements without the commercial pressure of a formal sourcing program.

The following is a suggested draft RFI document.

Request for Information (RFI)
Supply of XYZ

CLIENT BUSINESS AND CURRENT CONTEXT

Business Context, pressures / burning platform. Set the scene.

Our major focus and priority are to simplify all aspects of our business, remove substantial cost, and continue to operate safely.

OUTLINE OF BUSINESS THAT IS AVAILABLE TO PROSPECTIVE SUPPLIERS

Here we list volumes, timing of expiry of current contracts and also mention minimum qualification criteria that needs to be satisfied to win business such as safety, financial strength, experience, ability to meet our needs, and to adhere to our standard contract (refer to our website), etc.

DRAFT OUTLINE OF CRITERIA ON WHICH BUSINESS WILL BE AWARDED AT NEXT REQUEST FOR PROPOSAL (RFP) PROCESS

The RFP will contain a clear statement on how we will award business to the successful supplier. They will include:

- Minimum service level requirements including stock holding requirements, quantities, delivery times, etc.

- Minimum specification criteria—it may be better to specify the application and what we need the goods for, rather than get locked into a straitjacket/too restrictive a specification

- Any technology/innovation requirements

- Any key risks we want the supplier to absorb

- A proposal leading to an X per cent reduction within 12 months in the total cost impact to the business from 20XX spend of $X (thus including price, demand, specification and service level drivers); in recognition of this, client is open to consider an appropriate length of contract, a simplified commercial environment, and other criteria that the supplier may wish to propose.

INFORMATION SOUGHT FROM SUPPLIER

This includes company profile data or reference to website, why they would make a good supplier, confirmation they would be willing to participate in an RFP process and meet key commercial award criteria. We may also ask for indicative pricing for some specified items/services that would be included in an RFP to get a feel for the competitiveness of their offering.

CLOSE OFF WITH FORMALITIES

Who to write to, when, format, openness to consider questions, etc.

Depending upon responses received, the RFI document will help us eliminate potential suppliers so we speed up any RFP process, or it may narrow it down to one incumbent, in which case we can proceed straight to a renegotiation of existing terms.

Expression of Interest (EOI)

This is another *discovery* document (as in the RFI above) to engage the supply community and to test their interest in securing business that may be on offer. As in the RFI process, there are no contractual commitments that go with an EOI. However, it may help shorten or simplify the eventual sourcing program as one supplier may be a stand-out. In that event, and depending upon spend value, authority to proceed to a negotiated agreement leading to contractual commitment should come from the PSC. Alternatively, negotiations can proceed with other potential suppliers/respondents to the EOI to clarify aspects. It may give rise to solutions not previously considered and result in a sharpened CAC for an eventual formalised source program.

The results from an EOI can enhance the profile of procurement as it may introduce supplier feedback and recommendations to operations not previously considered. It can also be a strong engagement discussion on seeking internal business alignment on determining how they wish to proceed with the source program (e.g., proceed straight to award of business or follow a market-competitive process under an aligned CAC). Of course, if the decision is to proceed with a chosen supplier, there are aspects to consider such as budget constraints, fit for purpose considerations, whether the essential aspects of a typical CAC are met, and of course the requirements of a *sole source negotiation* need to be respected.

The following diagram is a draft pro forma EOI document.

EOI Discovery Template

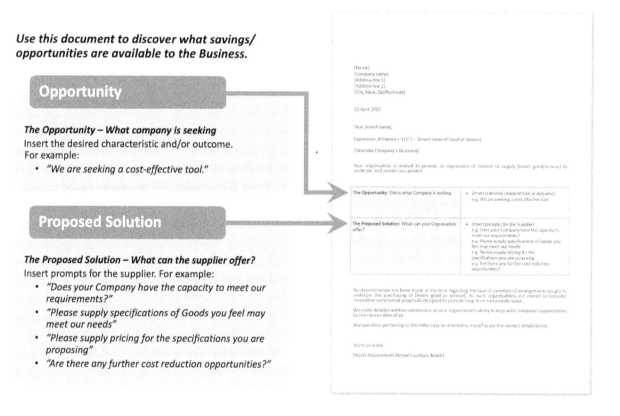

Use this document to discover what savings/opportunities are available to the Business.

Opportunity

The Opportunity – What company is seeking
Insert the desired characteristic and/or outcome.
For example:
- *"We are seeking a cost-effective tool."*

Proposed Solution

The Proposed Solution – What can the supplier offer?
Insert prompts for the supplier. For example:
- *"Does your Company have the capacity to meet our requirements?"*
- *"Please supply specifications of Goods you feel may meet our needs"*
- *"Please supply pricing for the specifications you are proposing"*
- *"Are there any further cost reduction opportunities?"*

Both documents serve to help the business understand the market better, understand who the potentially capable suppliers are, who to include or exclude from any upcoming source program and above all, shorten the process to contract award. The information generated from the process is usually powerful, informative and useful, assuming the right questions are asked.

CHAPTER 9
Negotiations

Before I introduce this chapter, let me say at the outset that what I can write in a few pages on the topic of negotiations cannot do justice to the subject, nor can I, given the number of existing professional experts in this field. Much has been written on this subject and it would be insincere of me to compete in this space.

That all said, I have been at the negotiating table many times (along with team members) dealing with a wide range of counterparties such as small to very large enterprises, those from different cultural backgrounds, sole source suppliers, as well as government organisations. There are strategies and tactics that I can offer from experience that can lead to successfully negotiated outcomes and I am happy to share these.

My focus here is on negotiations leading to contractual agreement for supply contracts.

As when going into an exam or a job interview, to be successful, preparation is key. Get that right and in my view, you are 50 per cent there. Preparation includes essential homework such as knowing your counterparty representatives, their strengths, leverage and how significant you are to them. Add the negotiating leverage of a BATNA, the ability to retain control of the process, being clear on your asks and position (this is informed by the CAC discussed earlier), being able to offer something in return to secure an outcome, possessing full negotiating authority, and working to a deadline; all of that together will, in most cases, be sufficient.

We can add more of course, such as thinking through the most difficult scenarios together with responses, practising for negotiations and anticipating that there will always be the X factor (the unexpected), hence the need to control the process.

My negotiating philosophy is not about "win-win", nor a "win-lose" but ensuring that terms are considered fair to both parties, that the outcome passes the competitiveness test, represents a good deal for both, that the contract terms are sustainable to avoid renegotiation or early termination, and the foundation for a good relationship can endure the term of the agreement. All this starts with a balanced contract. I do not subscribe to entering negotiations with a view to forming good relations as the primary motivation; that should be the outcome of successfully negotiated agreement reached between two parties acting on an arm's-length basis. The danger is that if relationship becomes key at the outset, the counterparty will pick up a *soft approach* and a compromised position may ensue that could lead to early termination due to lack of contract commercialism. This is not the same as saying I favour aggressive negotiations, rather, a professional level should be maintained throughout. Further, I am not proposing that the developed position through the CAC should not be demanding, nor the ask considered a stretch, as the mere fact the counterparty is meeting you at least ensures that a deal is possible.

Where to start? My starting point is to ensure control of the negotiation process and that can largely be achieved with a clear CAC, as articulated in the RFP and/or tender documents. There, the asks are very transparent, the basis of awarding business is clear, as is the timeframe to award business. It will be for the counterparty to argue against you if they wish to differ and offer compromises to achieve their aims.

Having a well thought out CAC achieves a number of negotiating aims:

- It keeps the negotiations confined to the important (i.e., what matters to the business)

- It can shorten the timeframe of negotiations as there is a boundary around the discussions to limited key matters

- As it has been signed off and supported by the business through the PSC (see below), it places procurement in control of the negotiation process as you can act with authority to agree or disagree to any aspect without the need to revert to a higher authority

- Those suppliers who have responded to the RFP/tender and selected to proceed to negotiations have already shown a strong alignment with meeting the key elements of the CAC and thus you are already substantially advanced in terms of deal finalisation.

Writing from experience, suppliers/counter parties, for the most part, will respect you more if you can show that you are very clear on what you want, you are working to a tight timeframe to award business, you have the negotiating authority to conclude a deal, you show you possess flexibility, and you are professional in your dealings. This to some may sound counterintuitive, especially when our asks may be demanding.

Suppliers do not value constant revisits of positions, the cost of adding time into the process, confusion of whether the real negotiating authority lies elsewhere in the business, or having an overly burdensome one-sided contract that is too onerous or has unbalanced risk allocation. Having the knowledge a decision will be made quickly, and dealing with people who are clear and know what they want, is a much easier proposition.

Earlier in this book, I introduced you to the establishment of a PSC and the essential purpose that it serves. One of those purposes is to approve negotiation strategies. There is no fixed content for these strategies as there are just too many variables at play, but typical strategy content would be created in PowerPoint, for example, and include:

- Description of what is under negotiation, counterparties, size of spend, duration of contract, criticality of product and supplier to the business, place of negotiations

- Negotiating strengths and leverage—ours and counter party(ies)

- Proposed team and leader, others and their proposed roles and what is known of the counter party(ies)

- Description of what a good deal could look like, trades to offer to achieve aims. In other words, be clear on negotiation objectives and outcomes sought and how they will be achieved in a true negotiating sense

- BATNAs; this is critical as it not only does indicate that the business has the option of an alternative, but it will also test members of the PSC to determine if in fact the position offered is acceptable. A suggested template on generating a BATNA position is shown below

- Confirmation of availability of key members of the PSC in the event a position must be tested and/or confirmed during negotiations

- Key asks including support required and or work required of PSC members before commencement of negotiations. For instance, this may be for the COO to speak to a member of their team to ensure key support is enlisted, or it may require the CEO to speak to a key contact to prepare the groundwork for potential change.

Once the strategy is approved, it places the negotiating team in a very strong position as the executive level support is there, and the delegated authority is apparent for concluding the deal.

BATNA Template

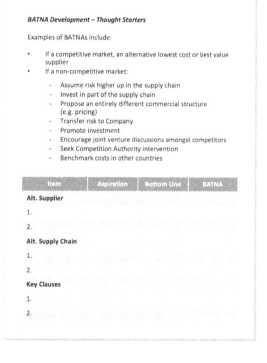

The purpose of the above template is to generate ideas that develop a BATNA position. In the absence of a competitive market, this requires some thought but nonetheless it is a useful exercise to follow and may generate the ideal solution to support a negotiation strategy.

Other points about negotiations include:

- It is always wise at the end of each session/day to note positions agreed upon, those that require further work and agreed timeframes to reach the next stage

- For more complex negotiations, reaching a significant milestone such as a *commercial term sheet*, documenting it and having it signed off by both parties is valuable. It then allows the respective parties to discuss other matters—be they legal aspects, contract implementation, supply chain or logistic details—with much of the essential hard work done

- One of the most time-consuming aspects in negotiations can be the finalisation of a legal contract. This can be due to a number of factors. It is usually driven by lack of balance in risk allocation between buyer and seller, or aspects which are very onerous, costly to administer, incompatible with the overall deal (e.g., size of contract, length of term, specification requirements and/or service levels) and so forth. There are of course some contracts that require time to ensure fair allocation of risk, some may be *one-off* in nature requiring many unique clauses. For the most part and largely speaking from my own experience, there are four ways that can be utilised to minimise time spent to conclude a contract:

  - Avoid a contract altogether and utilise a purchase or service order; adequate protection is provided and it can be used for purchases up to say a limit of A$150 000 (with due risk assessment carried out beforehand)

  - Standard contracts should be available on a company's website (e.g., under the procurement tab). This gives time for the counterparty to examine terms and indeed, this should be an integral part of the supplier qualification process. It goes without saying the lead negotiator should be familiar with all terms and be able to defend them

  - In supply contracts, there are three essential clauses that must be prioritised: quantities and supply security, pricing, and specification/service levels. If those are right, then other clauses can be negotiated to ensure balance and fair risk allocation. With supply security, careful attention should also be paid to the force majeure clause. The supplier should take ownership of the event and support the business in finding alternative sources to ensure continuity of supply. This is a particularly important clause for goods sourced overseas. The second level of priority in contract clauses which will vary depending upon the counter party and supply chain, will usually include warranties, liability and having the flexibility of a strong termination or contract dispute clauses. Going into contract discussions with clauses that fit into prioritisation levels will help the process of what can be more easily traded and those that cannot

- Introduce a number of "pick" clauses into clauses such as *liability, insurances* and other clauses that often take some considerable time to conclude. Thus, the standard contract would be the company position, however, provided a risk assessment is made on the contract, some relaxed positions on certain clauses can be offered provided this carries the approval of the legal team. This would be appropriate for easy to specify goods, or lower-value contracts.

A contract is, in essence, a risk management tool; it may be a simplistic view but keeping that in mind can be helpful in focussing on the important and avoid getting lost in excessive detail.

A few counterparties offer *non-negotiable terms* or *supplier terms*, evident in very large multinational organisations, where the onus falls on the purchaser to determine whether to accept positions or not. Experience dictates that fellow competitors in the industry or supply chain behave in a similar way, so buyer leverage may be limited. Professional legal support is essential in these circumstances, so the contractual risk position is clear to the buyer. Primary emphasis should still be placed on the three essential elements common to all supply contracts.

A common occurrence is negotiating with sole or single-source suppliers, which may place the buyer in a position of compromise and/or with little room for negotiation as no readily available BATNA exists. This situation can arise from a number of common scenarios. For example:

- Procurement is instructed to use one preferred supplier

- There is only one capable supplier in the market

- There is a market monopoly situation

- Only one supplier emerged from the tender/RFQ process

- A contract renegotiation

- In an RFQ scenario, where the message can be interpreted by the supply base as *"just give us a price; you have the business"*

Essentially, our leverage would appear somewhat limited and it may be difficult to satisfy the test of providing assurance that we are awarding business on sound commercial terms. We have no BATNA, so how should we approach this scenario? Consider the following options:

- The assumption going in is that procurement has a well-developed script to guide/focus supplier discussions, supported by the business through the PSC

- For the first three examples listed above, we have leverage in that the business needs a deal done despite the fact that there may only be one chosen supplier. We can say we have considered alternatives, and in fact that may be an outcome in future contracts, but for the time being we are pleased to continue with the supplier—subject to a successfully negotiated market-based contract. This would imply some level of homework; market data may be scant but what is not scant is the structure of a legal contract. That leads to our second leverage— we must assure we are in a position to award business on a sound commercial basis. If they want our business, we have to satisfy the test that the commercial deal is sharp but we also use our position to ask them to demonstrate it is commercial. An essential aspect of sole source contracts is to ask the supplier to justify price and demonstrate why it represents a good deal for the business

- We advise we can no longer afford to accept the contract pricing as we have done in the past. The focus is on commercialism and not on previously high service levels, nor on the quality of relationships. Commercialism trumps relationships

- We introduce phrases such as *fit for purpose, bronze plated not gold, transparency in dealings*

- We can also say (in the first and fourth examples above):

  - Given your incumbency and/or previous good service provided in the past, we are pleased to provide you with first-mover advantage to submit a commercial and competitive proposal that we can place in front of the business leadership for approval. The CAC will be . . . (list the four or five, including alignment with our cost-environment/cost-reduction objectives)

  - We are agnostic on supplier selection as the commercial test has to be satisfied as well as service and demonstration of capability; note that the decision is not just based on price, but on a TCI basis, so we encourage you to look at all cost drivers such as demand and service levels

  - We need cost transparency; thus, we know for example what market rates are for XYZ skill and the business white pages list any number of your competitors

  - Please provide your response by X and if your proposal is acceptable and meets the CAC, we can move to commercial award by XYZ date

  - If your proposal falls short, we will approach others; I am sure we both prefer is that this course of action is not followed, but our business condition may give us no alternative

- If it is a monopoly situation, clearly, we cannot say we will approach others (the counterparty will quickly call our bluff on that one). However, if we cannot afford to do business on previous terms negotiated, we should say that and then look towards some form of risk sharing arrangement such that once oil price or some other driver/exchange rate is >$X we can look to reopen terms. Some creativity should be advanced in a new and fairer pricing clause

- An RFQ is not a process that offers any form of assurance that we can award business on a *sound* commercial basis. Here we have two options. The first option is to issue an RFP and send the signal that this is open to competition (to preserve honesty in dealings, we can send it to a prospective supplier albeit unlikely that any deal is possible at the current time) or advise it is a pro forma one that will form the basis of future source programs. With a clearly stated CAC, they must ensure their proposal meets our objectives and thus it introduces commercialism into the process. It also gives us a base from which to negotiate if they fall short of the CAC. The second option is to issue the RFQ in name only and ensure their response meets a shortened CAC (namely *price ... extend to Total Cost of Ownership (TCO)/TCI, alignment with client business condition, fit for purpose solution, etc.*).

The keys still lie in business engagement for aligning our position, developing CACs that leave no room for the imagination, preparing to execute our BATNA (if not immediately, say after a year or so to develop an alternative supply chain), providing clear asks, doing our homework/essential preparation and maintaining professionalism in our dealings.

No two negotiations are the same—that is what makes it fun. One potentially complex negotiation is with people from different cultures as cross-cultural differences add a further level of complexity which should neither be overlooked nor ignored. Outside of Western cultures, the tendency is for counterparty teams to put forward a senior team that may not have the full negotiating authority to conclude, as they may have to take positions to higher levels in their respective organisations to finalise. So, the two cautions in cross-cultural negotiations are to show respect for the different cultures and to consider adding in additional time to conclude positions. High values are placed on relationships and that can work to the advantage of both parties at a later time should a contractual dispute arise. There is a significant amount more that can be said about cross-cultural negotiation, so I will leave it there save for saying as part of the preparation phase, an understanding of the counter party's culture will be a wise investment.

The last word on negotiations: This is an enormously intellectual exercise. It is a skill. There are many tactics required, and process and content are important, but with good preparation as indicated at the outset, you are 50 per cent there. The rest is up to the lead negotiator to exercise their skill, judgement and expertise. Practice for negotiations is essential to ensure confidence, assertiveness and process control by the negotiating team. When in the heat of the moment, never forget that when you agree to a counterparty demand or ask, ask for something in return. And lastly, do not be afraid to call for a "time out" if a break in proceedings may help see a way forward or provide an opportunity to reset the negotiating framework.

CHAPTER 10
Recommendation to Award

Recommendation to Award (RTA) is a topic worthy of a separate chapter as it is this document that represents the culmination of the sourcing and negotiation phases and it is where procurement presents the final project conclusions to the leadership team for a decision. It must be right, powerful in its communication, align with both the business direction—and most importantly—the work of the role of the leadership team.

The key question to be answered in the first part of the document is *what does this recommendation mean to me and my business?* In other words, *why* should I (say the CEO) accept it and *why* is it a good deal? What will it do to the business risk profile? What will it do to my cost profile, my safety performance, or my technology base?

So, the key information that should appear here is:

- Cost base measured on a TCI basis—Last year versus this year or next, depending if this spend category is the first time it has been sourced. How does it compare to my annual plan/forecast and what about any cost saving targets that we may have?

- Cash flow—Will it improve the business cash flow, and how? Do I have to invest money to establish the new relationship? When will I see the impact to costs and cash? Where will I see it in the financial statements?

- Safety—Will the supplier increase or decrease my safety risk profile in any way?

- Other risks—What else should I know, referring to supply chain management, experience with our business/industry, and their proven capabilities? If it is a new supplier, this may be important

- Further opportunities—For example, can the supplier introduce new technologies, improved packaging, technical support or other benefits the previous incumbent or competitors in the field could not?

The second part of the document should be focussed on *how* the savings will be achieved. Did we open an existing contract for renegotiation because we felt the present one was uncompetitive, or did we invite a number of suppliers to participate in our business, and based on key CAC, these were the best? One would need to state that the recommendation has the support of business operations/other.

We then conclude by saying, *how do we know it is a good deal and the best decision for our business?* This may include information on the market/trends and suppliers' support/alignment for our business in tough times through pricing/discounts and other key offerings. Again, a total cost perspective should be taken, and not just by comparing prices offered by competitors engaged in the sourcing program.

The RTA should be signed off by procurement and others who are involved in developing the recommendation.

This can all be done on a page; we do not need a lengthy PowerPoint presentation showing each supplier's bid, merits and so forth. The key is to get to the point quickly. We must never forget that those in senior leadership positions are busy people and do not have time to read lengthy reports, but they most certainly have time to read a one-page document that is well written and impacts their business.

An example of an RTA follows:

Recommendation To Award (RTA) Template

The Recommendation

Summarise the proposed recommendation.
Key inputs include:
- Who is the recommended supplier?
- What is the contract for?
- When will supply take place?
- What are the anticipated savings? (TCI basis)

Example recommendation:

"It is recommended that Supplier ABC be awarded a contract for the supply of [Insert Product]. Estimated savings will be $X compared to last year and $Y for forecast expenditure this year."

The Benefits Summary

Articulate how the business will benefit by implementing this recommendation and state why it is a good deal for the business. Summarise how the recommendation compares to the result of the sourcing exercise. This may involve a comparison of financial or non-financial criteria.

Examples of business benefits include:
- Cost savings
- Cash flow improvement
- Existing capital optimisation

Recommendation to Award Template

1. RECOMMENDATION
1.1. The Recommendation
Summarise the proposed recommendation. Key inputs include:
   a. Who is the recommended supplier, what is the contract for (i.e. what goods or services will they be supplying), when will supply take place, what are the anticipated savings. (TCI basis)

Examples of a recommendation are:
   b. "It is recommended that Supplier ABC be awarded a contract for the supply of *[Insert Product]*. Estimated savings will be $X compared to last year and $Y for forecast expenditure this year";
   c. "It is recommended that Supplier XYZ's existing contract for the supply of Maintenance Services is extended for another 2 years, as this will support the business in further reducing costs with a proven supplier. Anticipated savings are $X per annum against planned expenditure."

1.2 The Benefits Summary
   a. Impact to Business
      1. Articulate how the business will benefit by implementing this recommendation. Why you think this is a 'good deal' for the business. E.g. summarise how your recommendation compares to the results of your sourcing exercise. This may involve a comparison of financial or non-financial criteria;

Examples of business benefits include:
      1. Cost savings;
      2. Cash flow improvement;
      3. Existing capital optimisation;

Key area to highlight: How will the business benefit by implementing this recommendation?
If financial benefits, keep details brief and make sure there is a cross reference to the Economics section below, where you will provide further information.

   b. Economics
The recommended option's costs, how this compares to status quo, the results of the sourcing exercise and the indicative cost savings to the business (i.e. cost reduction, cash flow improvement). How do you know the preferred option is a good price (i.e. comparative responses during sourcing exercise)? What is forecast target cost savings under this option?

Key area to highlight: What is the savings potential and how is that calculation delivered? What does it mean to me and my business?

The template is self-explanatory. The key aspect to remember is that it is a document for top-line management, therefore, it must be presented with key business information.

CHAPTER 11
Measures

Most, if not all of you, the readers, will have heard of the expression, *what gets measured gets done*. There is a lot of merit in this saying, as from my experience, it has guided teams to focus on what is considered important (viz. the measures) and set the expectations and priorities of management. Measures take on even greater significance if selected ones form the basis of annual performance reviews and/or bonus calculations.

My only cautionary word is that having worked in a large corporation, I have seen that the focus and priorities of senior leadership can change quickly, particularly if a new business challenge comes along. For example, if *cost reduction* is the key performance indicator and then the business is faced with growth opportunities, the key metric changes to maximising production and with it, supply security. Old prioritised metrics then get forgotten until the same business challenge or strategic focus re-emerges. However, in procurement some things never change, and core measures should always be tracked and made visible.

I am confident most of you will be familiar with a number of traditional measures in procurement such as *savings generated, Delivery in Full and on Time (DIFOT), supplier defaults, inventory measures* and so forth. These remain valid and have their place, however, I would like to present new ones for consideration that are consistent with a high-performing procurement team. These measures are:

- *Total Cost Impact (TCI)*—This measures the direct impact a procurement team has on the cost profile of a business and hence its improved performance. See below for further detail supporting this important measure

- *Per cent of External spend prosecuted*—This measures how much of the external spend has been reviewed as well as challenged, and then subsequently renegotiated to improved commercial terms. See below for further detail on this measure

- *Average cycle time to initiate and conclude deals*—Speed is of importance to record a visible improvement to the bottom line. If a small cycle time is achieved, it implies that procurement processes relating to supplier engagement, negotiation and conclusion are under control, particularly its internal relationship with the business who are essential to deal approvals. Expanding upon this and with a bias towards outcomes and away from process measures, it completely changes the supplier engagement dynamic. Thus, instead of requesting the supplier to develop a response to an RFP/tender and thereby placing control of negotiations with the supplier, the business advises the market the basis it wishes to conclude business on, the timeframe to bring to closure and thus control vests with the enterprise

- *Number or per cent of suppliers who are aligned with client's business objectives/meet key commercial criteria*—This measure is a positive statement that signifies an active review of the supply base and where business is awarded on a TCI basis. A high percentage indicates excellence

- *Number of suppliers terminated through poor performance*—This shows the business is serious about not accepting poor service levels. A record, too, can be made of those placed on notice (one step before termination). This measure ensures that "cosy" relationships are not endured, but rather excellence in supplier performance and adherence to client expectations and business alignment exist.

TCI picks up all cost drivers (not just price) and includes specification changes, demand levers, relaxation of service levels and excludes exogenous factors such as measurable falls/rises to market prices (e.g., price of oil). Because the measure is TCI and traceable to the profit and loss account, it necessarily engages the operations and technical teams, as it is with them that the joint authority for concluding a deal lies. TCI also drives business alignment on CAC as the basis of supplier selection, deal outcome and consistency with business direction/plans. It thus broadens the authority of procurement to go beyond price as the sole lever to negotiate and provides procurement with a widened remit to conclude deals with a clear business mandate. It thus completely transforms the role of procurement as measured by traditional means.

Further, TCI brings procurement into the business as the team is measured on real enterprise performance measures—raising the team's profile and simplifying the value proposition of procurement's role to the organisation (viz. *bottom line impact* and away from *negotiated price point improvement from supplier responses*). This measure has the single greatest impact on transformation and setting procurement as a high-performing team. It directly traces procurement's value to the bottom line of the business. That value is what is important to a CEO and the senior leadership team and makes procurement's value proposition easy to define and transparent.

In the measure *per cent of external spend prosecuted*, high-performing teams aim for a high percentage each year and plan to cover the entire spend base at least once over a two- or three-year period. Markets change frequently and as much as long-term deals can have their place, new entrants can come in, thus placing pressure on incumbents providing opportunities to renegotiate terms to market.

Whilst not specifically mentioned above, the draft CPO Report to PSC in Chapter 4 (Procurement Steering Committee) highlights the measure of developing and refreshing new supply chain and other category strategies.

Of course, adopting the new measures does not preclude reporting and tracking of the team or individual tasks, such as supply chain performance, as may be apparent in traditional procurement models. The new measures described are more aligned with what the PSC would expect. As I indicate below, the application of TCO into decision-making is still valid, however, in times of ensuring rapid cost reduction, that measure becomes secondary to securing lower costs.

Total Cost of Ownership (TCO) is a sound principle when evaluating one product with another, or one supplier with another. Much has been written on its merits and is a valid measure in procurement's toolkit. I offer a caution when using the measure and that it should be used in conjunction with *fit for purpose* considerations to prevent over specification for a particular application. Also, in situations of a business transformation or turnaround, low-cost options should be a priority, simply because a business may not survive the near term. From my own experience, moving to lower-cost options has worked perfectly well and opens the business to previously untested products and suppliers. The business can always revert to preferred suppliers evaluated on a TCO basis once a business crisis has passed or the alternative product does not meet expectations.

The work of the role in procurement (and with it, related measures) will still embrace aspects such as contract management, management of key supplier relationships, purchase to pay processing, ensuring the business has fit for purpose procurement technology solutions and providing supply chain assurance. With a focus on expanding the role and profile of procurement and elevating its status within the organisation, new measures should be considered that align well with the expectations of the PSC.

Since the global outbreak of COVID-19, there is much that has been written that states the focus of procurement should not always be about money and profits, but rather the impact that commercial deals have on society as a whole. My contention is that procurement can do both—just as we can add dimensions such as environmental factors, sustainability and safety into measurement systems and make them an integral part of CAC. They don't have to be mutually exclusive as businesses that demonstrate excellence in safety, environment, health and well-being of employees, and have presence in the community are profitable as well. Knowingly accepting suboptimal commercial deals is incompatible with procurement excellence.

CHAPTER 12
Strategy

Perhaps a more appropriate place to discuss the subject of procurement strategy would be in Chapter 1 (Getting the Fundamentals Right), however, a few concepts required discussion before considering this topic. A strategy is always a good place to start when setting the business in a new direction.

To some, the development of a procurement strategy may be a daunting prospect but when broken down to its key elements, it is no different to many other strategies. Namely, understand your baseline, know where you want to go and define success, determine the gaps, describe a plan on *how* you are going to get there (in effect the *strategy*), and list the measures that will test the success of progress and value achieved.

The following is a list of resources required to develop strategy:

- Spend profile analysis – discussed in Chapter 16 (Technology)

- An understanding of *where we are now*—this includes a listing of measures comparing business performance with leading performance, a listing of what procurement is doing well, and what is deficient. This covers sourcing measures, transactional efficiency, number of team members relative to spend under management, and much more. It also itemises supporting technologies in use, their effectiveness, consideration of how procurement is perceived both within the business and externally, as well as procurement's role in aspects such as sustainability, carbon footprint, and how well procurement supports business goals and aspirations

- An understanding of *where we want to be*—realistic goals of what can be achieved in a one-year or two-year timeframe. What are the aspirations? Do we want to be a leading organisation? What technologies do we need to help achieve our goals? Against the listing of baseline performance above, where do we want to go?

- Then the hard part; namely to define the actions, activities required to get there, assign accountabilities to respective leaders and determine the cost of getting there. This is the opportunity to identify what practices need to stop or to change, those to simplify, and those to implement. What are the key aspects that are going to make the biggest difference and have the greatest immediate impact? A determination needs to be made of what the strategy's business benefit will be and how long it will take to realise the full potential of the strategy

- Identify the measures to track performance.

A question that needs to be answered is *who* determines where to take the organisation in a procurement sense. Clearly this would be the accountability of the CPO, but they cannot do it alone. Strong business support will be required and as a minimum the PSC will be involved and have authority over the business direction. Should there not be a PSC, then it would fall to the EXCO. This is the opportunity for the CPO to shine and demonstrate their leadership capabilities to influence business direction, show how procurement can impact performance, set a compelling vision and showcase the value potential of the strategy.

A strategy is a useful tool to guide the business as it sets itself on a new pathway. It also provides clarity to team members on where the business is heading and is a useful tool to help new team members quickly familiarise themselves with the organisation and their role to achieve success. Developing a strategy is a valuable team-building exercise and can be especially useful piece of work when a new leader is appointed. It is also useful in building and ensuring sound relationships with operations and other key user groups as they can assist in defining perceived gaps and what their priorities are, thus influencing strategic direction.

Strategies can also get out of date quickly—particularly with the advent of new technologies, a change in business circumstances and other major unplanned events that may have a detrimental impact to business, such as COVID-19. These events may require shelving certain aspects in the strategy, pending resolution of other critical business priorities which will direct procurement's attention. In fact, in times of ambiguity, strategies must be agile as priorities can shift on a weekly, if not daily basis.

Therefore, as a minimum, an annual refresh of strategy is preferred and once a strategy is in place, the work to update it will be easier and will help fine-tune over- or under-ambitious goals and set new targets and priorities that assure strong alignment with business goals.

I have not listed typical measures to identify to compare with *best or leading practice*. Typically, they would be effectiveness and efficiency measures (these can be numerous). The more difficult part is to gain access to what leading practice actually represents and whether it is an appropriate metric for the business to use. This is where the use of external consultants may provide expert advice and support. If used, consultant input can provide legitimacy to strategic direction. The alternative approach is simply to put a stretch target for each measure, however, the actions required to get there still need to be articulated and assigned as part of the strategy document. Above all, the direction of procurement must align with that of the business and not place a stretch target for the sake of it.

A word on *vision*. It is always valuable in setting strategy to have a view of the end goal, to know what success looks like, and to know when a business has reached its full potential. Of course, in the modern, dynamic world we are in, that end goal is always extended simply because of technology and other global developments that change any original assumptions made. Events beyond the control of the business can suddenly become a new priority and hence agility, resilience and flexibility become the new norm of the organisation.

When setting strategy, a procurement vision does not always have to be *world's best*, which is very difficult to define in any event, but it should incorporate certain minima, namely:

- Be one, fully integrated with the business and not in a service capacity; in this way, procurement can have direct influence and impact on the profit and loss account, have peer status with operations, and be rewarded for commercial outcomes. Ensure sound relationships with and have direct access to the CEO, the COO and the CFO of the business

- Adopt technologies that add value to the process, eliminate transactional inefficiencies and enhance the control environment leading to greater effectiveness

- Develop and implement an annual procurement plan, adopt the right measures and report on progress frequently, ideally to a PSC

- Resource the team with capable people

- Eliminate bureaucracy, have requisite governance, and adopt efficient processes that place the business in control of source programs.

Personally, I have always found a strategy useful, as often *we don't know what we don't know* and going through strategy development can help lift the eyes of the business to the outside world, away from insular thinking and help steer the organisation to achieve business plan goals more quickly.

.

CHAPTER 13
Supplier Relationships, Contract and Vendor Management

Once a sourcing program is complete and business is secured through a contract, then the important facet of work begins, namely, the implementation of the contract, moving to managing supplier relationships, and contract and vendor management.

This is work done usually in the background—it has little visibility and if things go smoothly and without the need for escalation, then it is likely to remain that way. It is essential, critical work and if ignored, the efforts required to regain stability can be huge, consume a lot of management time and worse, it is a non-value-adding activity to the extent the business should never have got into that position in the first instance, and detracts it from other priorities. So, the clear recommendation is to ensure this work is seen to be important within the procurement function, it is valued, and reporting metrics are made visible to the team members on a team noticeboard or equivalent to highlight the activity.

It would be incomplete of me to ignore the global COVID-19 pandemic, which apart from causing massive supply disruptions and major business survival challenges, places a priority and emphasis on supplier relationships like never before. Supplier agility and resilience are now key, resulting in an increased emphasis on local suppliers and the nearshoring of services. This is discussed more in Chapter 14 (Supply Chain Management).

COVID-19 may make some of what I write below a little less relevant in today's world as we steer our way through a crisis, but stability will return and does not detract from the importance of relationship, contract, and vendor management as key aspects of the work. They are relevant regardless where we are in the economic or business cycle.

Also, before I do go further, the subject of *strategic suppliers* often comes up and whether the concept exists in practice. Suppliers of critical raw materials, equipment, specialised outsourced expertise necessary to support an operation and sole suppliers can all fit into this category. If any of them were to "fall over" and go into bankruptcy then clearly this would place the business under enormous strain as it can place production and the efficient running of the business at risk. Most organisations have such supply relationships, and sometimes the risk is spread amongst two or more suppliers, but that is not always possible—consider power and water suppliers that are part of a grid system.

My contention is that the word *strategic* may not be the correct description; however, strategic suppliers are certainly very important and indeed, some special pricing or support is offered to the business through them, compared to that provided by other suppliers. That may not make them strategic though. Also, it is not uncommon for suppliers to commit to product and technology development and offer the business the first opportunity to trial or utilise these for competitive advantage. This can be extended to *joint development of technologies* and these relationships certainly make these suppliers valuable. They can be considered part of the business so their management does require special attention and needs some dedicated, skilled resources applied to the relationship. The word used to describe these relationships is less important than the action itself of managing them so that intended contractual obligations flow from that secured through negotiation.

My experience is that these relationships need both parties to view the relationship equally to drive maximum value from it. One must not forget that it is still a commercial contract. Suppliers can still exhibit opportunistic behaviours; they do not always succumb to changing demands placed on them and will be the first to ask for price increases if market dynamics change or if their supply chain is broken. If the supplier adopts a new strategic direction, the business will be the first to share or feel the pain of the risk. This brings into question the word *strategic* and hence I avoid using it, and instead consider them as important or valued. The same would be said of relationships that are described as *partnerships*—those too must be managed as they are commercial contracts.

For these valued contracts and relationships, it is appropriate to have a simple suite of measures applied, followed up by performance reviews. The business does not want these relationships to fail, so some active management is required. The key lagging indicator would be *Delivery in Full, on Time and within Specification (DIFOTIS)*. Any process defaults would be followed up quickly to prevent their recurrence. The real key lies in taking a future view to understand what may be coming up in the horizon that presents an opportunity or a risk to the business. These reviews should take place at three- or six-month intervals, depending on the situation, and would involve senior representation from the business and the supplier. If the focus of the relationship is on technology or on intellectual property, then clearly the measures would differ.

Key aspects for discussion should include:

- Supplier and business forecast of activity in the following review period. Consider seasonal changes, abnormalities, and shut down maintenance programs and their impact to both parties

- Any new capital investment that will be installed and its impact to operations

- Any microeconomic or macroeconomic forecast trends that will impact either party's business

- Improvement work underway to simplify supply chain management (both parties)

- Any new technologies that will be introduced by either party that will improve supply chain aspects

- Review of past period performance and any close out of actions (both parties).

Whilst this may not solve or predict all unforeseen problems, at least proactive management is in place to deal with known aspects and prevent surprises.

Good supplier relationships should not get in the way of good contract management. What I mean here is that if a supplier defaults (referring to a serious issue), a formal contract default notice should be issued to the vendor and to ask for rectification within a prescribed period. This should happen regardless of the quality of the relationship. In that way the matter is formally communicated, and corrective action can be managed. It is easy to allow the supplier to correct an issue, but its seriousness and urgency may be hidden from senior management levels of the supplying entity. The result may be that the event recurs or it is not corrected to the requisite level of satisfaction.

Relationships can still be professional and what this action demonstrates is the contract manager is doing their job without fear or favour to any party and acts in the best interests of the business.

Another type of contractual relationship is a profit-sharing one. I generally do not favour these as they require an enormous amount of work to administer and manage the tracking of metrics. Both parties seek to maximise the position for their own benefit, and they can quickly fail if the metrics designed provide no commercial benefit to either party. Above all, my experience is that they tend to lack commercialism and do not often drive the intended behaviours. They can of course work but my strong preference is that supplier obligations and relationships should not need incentives to perform. Suppliers should possess the requisite capability at the outset, hence the reason they were selected. I contend the opposite should apply, namely, that failure on key supply chain or performance metrics should lead to early termination. The business reason for establishing these type of contracts needs to be carefully examined and consideration given to alternative and simpler structures to achieve relationship and commercial goals.

However, where an incentive type contract can and does function well is in capital works, which I have covered in Chapter 7 (Services Procurement). In summary, if a project is completed earlier then a planned or a specified date, then value can accrue to the business in an NPV sense as revenue will start to flow earlier from built increased capacity and earlier than planned production starts. Further, there may be lower-budgeted capital costs and so forth; to work, capable project managers from both the supplier and business side will be required to ensure safety issues are not overlooked, there are no shortcuts taken, specification minima are adhered to and the business representative is on hand to deal with queries quickly and effectively. Incentives like these do work and can drive the right behaviour.

For all other contracts, the level of management will vary depending on their size, frequency of transactions and relative importance to the business. The key metric will be DIFOTIS and any process defaults should be quickly followed up on to prevent recurrence. Other aspects to manage include whether lead times can be shortened, as well as the number of process defaults and countermeasures. In the latter case, if poor performance continues, termination should be considered as otherwise it is a reflection that too much management time is taken up on a non-performing supplier to the detriment of the business.

Some businesses hold an annual supplier award ceremony where awards are given to the best suppliers based on their performance over the preceding 12 months. I hold no particular views on this activity; my preference though, is to simplify this process, post some positive review comments on particular suppliers on the company's website (under the procurement tab) so all can read praise provided and in addition, offer the opportunity to grow and extend the contractual commitments with the supplier concerned. It may also provide an incentive for other suppliers to equal or better their performance.

Accounts Payable and Payment Terms

I have not prioritised this important aspect of the procurement process as often the accounts payable team does not fall under its remit, and usually it sits within accounting and finance. I personally have no strong preference where it should belong—I do know that it can be a source of frustration amongst the supply community if payment terms are missed or are unduly long, particularly amongst small and sole-proprietor businesses. It is for that reason I favour profiling suppliers into two broad categories where payment terms are concerned. The first category is the standard business practice of 30 days and that would encompass the majority of vendors. For small businesses I would promote a 15-days-or-less payment cycle—small enterprises form the backbone of an economy and do not have the financial muscle to accept or be subject to extended terms. These would cover many local suppliers supporting an enterprise. In addition, some industries work on a strict, non-negotiable seven-day payment cycle, notably in the shipping and power industries, and little flexibility is offered. Naturally, if shortened payment terms are required then some form of benefit should be offered in return (e.g., advantageous pricing). Post the GFC in 2008, it was common to extend supplier payment terms to 60 days or more to preserve cash flow but ultimately that action results in higher pricing given the increased risks involved.

Also, it is not uncommon for accounts payable to be outsourced to an offshore Business Process Outsourcing (BPO) provider—my preference is to retain this as an in-house function as it allows queries to be dealt with promptly and to retain goodwill with the local supply community. Naturally if it is outsourced, managing key measures and ensuring vendor queries are dealt with promptly would be essential priorities in the relationship.

The key is to manage accounts payable well with whatever solution is preferred, including technologies adopted to support the process. If not, the risk profile of dealing with the business increases and will result in disaffected suppliers and higher pricing of goods to compensate for the risk.

In summary, supplier relationships are important, they are a source of value, they need to be managed as do the supporting contracts, and they do take time and effort. The importance of this essential work should not be understated.

CHAPTER 14
Supply Chain Management

Supply chain management can either be a topic that is below the radar because everything is under control, or a hot, critical topic when it is not under control. For example, if a stock outage exists or an essential item for business continuity is close to zero holding, it becomes a number one priority for procurement and for the business to address.

When procurement succeeds in overcoming supply deficiencies, its status within the business can skyrocket and such is the value that is placed on supply security. It is then that the business is reminded of the value that procurement can bring to an organisation.

In fact, when considering risks that procurement has to manage, this would be one of, if not *the* highest risk. The risk is compounded if the predominate source of supply is from a foreign country; as in that circumstance one must deal with country risk, industry risk, enterprise risk, transportation risk and possibly a language risk as well.

At some stage in a business lifecycle, it is inevitable that a stock outage will result, many times because of an unforeseen and sudden change in the fortunes of a supplier or market dynamic. It is therefore not an uncommon experience and when it arises, business resources need to be tasked with overcoming the issue as a top priority.

Supply chains can become broken for a number of reasons, not all of which can be foreseen despite best efforts. A broken supply chain can result from events such as:

- A strike at a supplier plant

- A sudden increase in export tariffs imposed by a foreign jurisdiction driving production curtailments or unsustainable price increases globally

- Supplier plant outages

- Pressure placed on many businesses to expand and not enough capacity in the supply chain to meet requirements, as was witnessed prior to the GFC when suppliers could not keep up with customer demand

- Wars and famines in foreign jurisdictions, where a few certain products are in huge local and global demand and the supply chain system cannot cope.

Consider the COVID-19 global pandemic and the massive business and supply chain disruption it has created. Relationship management has never been so important, both within an organisation such as between the EXCO or the PSC, as well as externally with supply chains. To avoid disruption and maintain executive support, procurement leaders must recognise the importance of their role in the business—offering financial or operational support to their tier one, two, and in some cases tier three or four suppliers, whilst maintaining working capital within their own organisation. Suddenly the value that procurement brings is redefined, be it by cost or supplier agility and resilience, resulting in an increased emphasis on local, more agile suppliers and the nearshoring of services.

Once the supply shortages have been overcome and a level of normality returns to the business, it is appropriate to conduct a root-cause analysis or other problem-solving technique to identify how and why the shortage arose, countermeasures to put in place to avoid recurrence, and to ensure role accountabilities are clarified so that people are left with no doubt as to what their continuing role will be to ensure a smooth supply chain.

What usually happens under this scenario is that once the problem has been overcome and supply chains remain stable for a long period, the accountability, importance and focus on supply chain assurance becomes deprioritised until it happens again.

My contention is that supply chain assurance should *never* be off the radar as a business priority, as there are always improvements to be made. New and innovative solutions present themselves frequently from third-party providers and also, if nothing else, there are costs and risks involved: a) through an unexpected outage, b) the cost of excessive stock holdings, c) costs of transportation and storage, d) costs and risks of trialling an alternative supplier, and e) the flow-on impact to potential excessive working capital.

So, how do we ensure this is kept at the forefront of the business and recognised as a critical measure, just as we monitor profitability, return on capital employed, margins and so forth?

To answer that, the first question that needs to be answered is, *who in the business is accountable for supply chain assurance?* More often than not, the answer will be procurement. If that is the case, then it must appear as a critical measure for the CPO and be reported and tracked as a line item for the PSC to review.

What complements this measure are several aspects not normally considered within the remit of a CPO's brief:

- A forecasting capability, factoring in current inventory levels, future demand and usage, knowledge of delivery cycles, storage capabilities, reliability of delivery cycles, lead times and so forth. In other words, there is some considerable work involved

- Keeping abreast of current microeconomic and macroeconomic events, changes, as well as the local political and geopolitical landscape. There may be a strike at an overseas port impacting exports, tariff regimes may change, changes and potential changes of governments may result in banning certain exports, there may be local issues, a change in law regarding transportation safety may be introduced, or in other words, a host of matters that can suddenly expand into a problem

- The above point considers physical flows but there may be trends in financial markets that can impact supply chains. For example, sudden currency devaluations that make production in offshore countries uneconomic, interest rate increases may force business closures, or a country's borrowings may pass a limit that causes it to go bankrupt.

The list is not exhaustive, but these are all types of events that can manifest themselves in supply chain disruptions.

Finally, but by no means least, when a situation arises such as a global pandemic such as COVID-19 or a GFC event, the prudent CPO in such circumstances should do the following:

- Advise senior leadership of the impact of the event to the business and its supply chain

- Develop a strategy to preserve business continuity

- Begin the qualification of new supply chains

- Develop product substitution strategies

- Build strategic stockpiles

Of course, this work will be delegated in part to those who are accountable for individual spend categories. The clear accountability lies with the CPO though, who is on hand to ensure the right work is done by the team and brought to the attention of the PSC if required.

The ideal scenario is that no one business is totally reliant on one supply chain to assure its continuity of production or output. If that scenario does exist (and it is not uncommon for a business to have a sole supplier for one product such as fuel), the clear strategy should be to have a second or third qualified supplier to turn to in the event of an emergency.

Supply chain assurance, like contract, supplier and vendor management, logistics and a few other skills usually sit with a procurement team and are not skills in themselves that are highly prized or valued by a business. The work is invisible and no one in the business acknowledges anything—especially if all is under control and no matters become escalated to senior leadership.

Here is what I would advise to ensure this work and these skills are recognised: Firstly and importantly, there is the role of the PSC where on an annual basis, the strategies for these areas should be presented to demonstrate that the risks and opportunities are known and are managed, counter measures and activities are in place to control them and above all to demonstrate to the senior leadership that this work is well managed. As they are business-critical matters, it provides the opportunity for the senior leadership to provide further input and guidance. In addition, ensuring support for this work is important as we are talking about potentially serious risks the business may encounter and a potential significant loss of value if they are mismanaged. Be assured this action will certainly be of interest to the PSC.

The second way to ensure requisite profile for this work is through the CPO, namely advertising and celebrating successes with key groups directly impacted by good work done. It will keep the work visible, and the business will be aware of the critical support procurement provides for the efficient running of the business.

CHAPTER 15
Governance

Good governance is essential to good business and few would dispute that.

Following on from that statement, over-governance would not represent good practice; it is costly to maintain and support, generates much work, requires excessive documentation, does not separate out the important from the less so and generates bureaucracy. Further, it can slow down decision-making and add complexity that serves little value-adding activity to work streams.

The ability for a business to make quick decisions should be paramount.

Few would dispute what is written in the second paragraph, and the following question and challenge: *How much over-governance exists in your business? Can we define what effective governance looks like?*

Where I am coming from in this chapter, is to say, *governance is essential and must be respected and adhered to; the aim is to ensure compliance with no process defaults.* Over-governance, excessive controls, and lengthy documentation requirements should be challenged. Experience also tells me it is far easier to design complex systems than it is to design simple ones, just as it is more difficult to write a one-page executive summary on a major project than it is to write a 20-page one.

In a procurement sense, the minimum requirements for governance usually centre around the following:

- For sourcing programs, they are not only authorised but also ensure there is an open, transparent process allowing every participant an equal opportunity of winning the business. This may be a particularly important point when dealing with local communities

- All business awards are made by the appropriate level of authority following a recommendation in a prescribed format

- There is a supporting document that covers the contractual relationship (a contract, a purchase or service order) commensurate with the level of spend

- Stricter levels of controls surround sole sourcing programs for the principal reason that no open competitive process is followed. See below for more detail on sole source awards.

One aspect that usually does receive high-profile status is *sole source awards* that do not follow due process. For my money, I am not particularly concerned if a contract is awarded to a sole source vendor provided due process is respected and followed. Our avenue to ensure due process is the PSC and we must justify the reason for sole source to that group. If the pre-authorisation is provided, then all is fine. We need to remind ourselves that following a sole source award may in fact be good business—it may speed up commencement of supply or work, it may from a total cost perspective be the optimal or it may be a reflection of the particular capabilities the supplier may have.

Another potential area of business risk can arise from sourcing products, materials and services from emerging economies. Compared to First World countries, standards of Health Safety and Environment (HSE) or commercial law practice may not align well and will most certainly be different. Further, there may also be the risk of corruption. Naturally, good due diligence is required, and it places emphasis on the importance of the supplier qualification process which should be made visible on the company's website (procurement tab) and should be a requirement for all suppliers to complete and satisfy requisite minima.

The best way to think of requisite governance from a design perspective, is to envision a value-adding process, not a bureaucratic one, nor one that slows down decision-making. Thus, having multiple process steps and sign-offs at each stage and requiring documentation to be in a prescribed format adds minimal value as the *objective* of governance is lost.

As quoted from https://aicd.companydirectors.com.au/, the website of the Australian Institute of Company Directors (AICD), *"Effective governance structures allow organisations to manage their affairs with proper oversight and accountability, to create value for shareholders or members through sound investment and innovation, and provide accountability and control systems commensurate with the risks involved."*

When considering the minimum requirements that address good governance, as described above, consider the following which have been discussed in earlier chapters:

- Commercial Award Criteria—Within that, there is absolute clarity on how business will be awarded—and by its design, has absolute business support. That would certainly satisfy a fairness perspective by the supply community

- The Procurement Steering Committee—Its agenda is to authorise sourcing programs such as sole source and open competitive ones for the following month. Only authorised work gets done, and again that would satisfy the transparency rule

- The recommended format for awarding business through the RTA documentation—There the project is closed off by a recommendation to the appropriate signing authority which includes essential process steps compliance

- A standard legal contract is utilised within the business (as found on the company's website), as well as standard purchase and service order documentation.

All of these address good governance.

Experience shows that complexity arises when there is lack of clarity on how business will be awarded and in turn, this leads to many countermeasures that are put in place through governance processes. For example, many RFPs that are placed in the market that state, *proposals are invited from capable suppliers for the supply of X. We are looking for innovation, etc.* but this lacks the clarity of *how* a decision will be made. Is it on price or is it on a range of factors, and which ones are more important than the others?

Further complexities arise where a sourcing program is run inviting potential suppliers to participate but a decision/preference has already been made by operations as they do not want to introduce process risk—there may even be a relationship established by the business. That would lack business integrity as it represents dishonesty to other participants in the process as they were never going to be given an opportunity to win the business. The CAC would counter these concerns, as would the PSC, in authorising the following month's sourcing programs. It is also the role of the CPO, who would highlight risks where business personnel would be identified that may not be agnostic to supplier selection (refer to Chapter 4 on the PSC).

A further area of concern may arise through inadequate or poor follow up with potential suppliers who may have lost out in business award. The reasons should be stated, where their failings were evident and factors to consider when the sourcing process is run again.

To strengthen the role and purpose of procurement, clear statements should be placed on the company's website under the procurement tab, including:

- Integrity statement

- Code of business ethics

- Independence

Spot audits can be carried out at any time to verify process compliance with selected contracts or sourcing activities. This is consistent with the *simplicity* theme and not designing an overly heavy level of documentation to support compliance programs.

And on a final note, by keeping things simple, it can lead to speedy business decision-making and above all by ensuring professionalism in business dealings, it will engender trust with the supply community and suppliers will want to do business with you, further promoting a healthy competitive environment.

CHAPTER 16
Technology

In the introduction to this book, I mentioned I would provide only a light touch on this topic as quite frankly, the range of matters and technologies that can be discussed are huge and are best left to the experts as well as suppliers who can offer particular technologies.

Arguably though, this should be one of the most important chapters in the book because any business that is not seeking to deploy the capabilities of e-commerce to the maximum extent could very well be wearing a high cost of inbuilt inefficiency. Digital transformation projects (intelligent workflows for sourcing and procurement) are now accelerating in use. These represent a step change to past technology applications and the full business impact understood as it can, for example, ensure that procurement teams have a clear visibility of their supplier base which is so important in supply chain management. They can also support the removal of embedded bureaucratic processes thus enabling greater collaboration across all functions to drive sustainable results. With an enhanced control environment and elimination of manual work, the role of procurement becomes more rewarding.

There are many technology providers who offer these services—each one different—so it is best I leave that to them, other than saying I fully endorse their use in the business.

The CPO owes it to their team to deploy technology to simplify work practices, automate transactions, and provide tools that produce information to assist and support people in the work of their roles. These are all *must haves* for a high-performing 21st century procurement team.

Of course, as with all technologies, it is how you use them and what you do with the information that can be extracted from their use that matters. And, technologies must work; there is no value in having installed the latest technology only to discover it does not provide the fully intended benefits or requires further costs to meet particular needs. Technology selection and implementation require thought and effort.

Apart from what I have noted above, one of the critical technologies to have at the disposal of the CPO and their team is the ability to generate a spend profile analysis of the business, namely spend analytics. This can provide incredibly powerful data and can not only show where the money is spent, but also by whom, to whom. It builds a picture on the supplier base, and the frequency and size of transactions. And from it, numerous conclusions can be drawn.

Having powerful data at the disposal of a CPO can enhance the role significantly. From it, inefficiencies can be highlighted, opportunities identified, and insights provided into the business that are not considered when reviewing business financial performance. It also allows priorities to be set and where costs can be removed from the business, both of which will be of interest to PSC members.

The data can also be helpful from a financial control perspective and can provide information to show where costs have been incurred without a supporting purchase or service order. It can point to where spend or supplier consolidation can be considered, and it can point to "rogue" suppliers and/or maverick spend—suppliers with whom no contract exists or those outside suppliers authorised from the conclusion of sourcing programs.

A potential source of value that can be generated from spend analysis is considered to lie in supplier consolidation, namely the cutting of the number of suppliers, the concentrating of volume in fewer prospective vendors and the leveraging of bigger volumes to secure a price reduction.

From my experience, this takes a lot of hard work for minimal, if any, benefit. Spend is often relatively insignificant, suppliers do not offer price reductions easily through higher volumes (often this can be a threat to their business as their marketing risk can increase through a smaller customer base) and then there is the risk of managing disaffected suppliers who may be reluctant to re-engage with the business. Also, the number of suppliers to a business is not in itself an indicator of anything particularly good or bad; in fact a spread of suppliers amongst local communities can be seen to be good. The counterargument lies in the number of relationships to support. If the supplier consolidation route is followed, the keys lie in explaining the benefits expected to accrue to both parties and exercising great care to not alienate the supply base you may rely on in the future.

Similarly, on that theme, I have often been challenged to secure better pricing through the mantra of *leveraging volume to secure a low market price* (i.e., consolidate spend across plants and group businesses to leverage this into price reduction). In this instance and example, I am talking of significant market volumes.

To be honest, this can work and has achieved results, but a deeper understanding of market and supply chain dynamics needs to be undertaken before adopting this strategy. The number of suppliers in the market, their location, their capacity, whether items are easy to specify or are indeed common across the organisation, and whether suppliers are producers or intermediaries all have a bearing. Many suppliers may see it as a threat as they are denied selling to other profitable markets. If however, it is the difference between keeping a plant at full production or not, or real economies do exist from the higher contract volumes, then the opportunity for success is greater. The issue that needs to be understood is *why would a supplier want to give away margin and how much can you reasonably expect?* Hence, an understanding of how the market, the supplier and supply chain function are all prerequisite work.

What does secure better pricing and resultant lower costs is a well-developed CAC and following the market engagement strategies outlined in Chapter 6 (Sourcing).

It is essential to invest in other technologies that can provide insights and access to data such as:

- Market analysis that support category management development and strategy

- Inventory management that can support sound inventory control practices such as line item stock turnovers, items that have not moved for six months or more, supplier delivery performance, catalogue management to support data cleansing such as duplicate, incorrectly recorded items or those that show no records

- Unfulfilled purchase and service orders

- Items purchased without a supporting purchase or service order

- Asset management information such as equipment utilisation, equipment duplication, idle assets, repair history and spend per equipment item.

My list does not do justice to all those available and demonstrating their full capabilities, but you will glean a flavour of the sort of information that supports productive work, to the extent that if these are not under consideration for a procurement team, it can only lead to suboptimal performance and thus constrain the full potential of the team.

Drivers of having the right technologies are:

- Eliminating unproductive, labour-intensive work

- Simplifying work

- Adding value to the work of the role

- Speeding up or automating transactional work

- Supporting sound decision-making

- Supporting an enhanced control environment

- Providing information that can provide the necessary insights to lift role or team performance.

My preference is to have technologies, where possible, integrated with the main business system—otherwise duplication of data entry will occur and with it the risk of errors of recording or omission. A clear example of this would be to have a stand-alone inventory system (one that is not fully integral with the business ERP). It may well be the reporting functionality of the stand-alone system is what drives the technology selection, but the additional cost of inefficiency in duplication and reconciliation to the core ERP system data can outweigh any benefits.

BPO can be a valuable part and extension of the core procurement team providing a specialised resource on services such as market research, supplier profile analysis, documentation and report writing, to name a few. If used, it frees up the time of the procurement team's leadership to focus on strategy and essential core aspects of the role. It is undoubtedly a value-adding service and like with all major suppliers, it is a relationship that needs to be managed, with correct KPIs applied and the service frequently reviewed to ensure original and core objectives are achieved.

As BPO providers are usually offshore, distance should not be seen as a barrier as technology can overcome this aspect. The critical issue over and above KPI management is to ensure the BPO provider is seen as an integral part of the core business from a cultural and organisational alignment perspective. Not all businesses require the services of a BPO provider, but for high-performing procurement teams, acquiring and training capable capacity may be a constraint to delivering strategic objectives. The services of BPO providers can not only address this aspect, but they can be installed relatively quickly (after appropriate due diligence) as it is a competitive landscape with many organisations operating in this space.

The other essential area to invest in would be to have a procurement website (as part of the main business one) where procurement policies, standard contracts, supplier qualification criteria (which would include aspects on HSE, financial strength and other capabilities' minima), team structure, roles and team photographs can be stored. This not only adds to transparency with the supply community but can also save in much paperwork with RFP and tender documentation as references can be easily made for suppliers to access. References would also be made to the organisation's HSE policies and requirements expected of the supply base in meeting and aligning with business expectations.

From an intranet perspective, I would store scopes of work issued to suppliers, developed CACs used, reports generated, protocols, pro forma material and other related matters that may need to be accessed quickly, referred to later or leveraged into new documentation.

Most technologies can be justified both by the provider and the business— though the business case needs to carefully examine the real savings and benefits that they provide and how quickly the transparency of the benefit will transfer to the bottom line. It is incumbent on the procurement team to identify which technologies are required for their teams and ultimately the business. Their justification beyond the business case would be to assess if there is a true business need and once installed, review it frequently to determine whether the original intended value still exists. I say this because the technology field is constantly changing and advancing; there are new market entrants and what is in place may become quickly outdated.

I reflect on my own experience, too, where some incorrect technology selections have been made and/or where improved management of the technology provider would have added value to business needs, or where a switch to an alternative provider would have been more beneficial and less costly in the long run. I share this as learning from past mistakes is not only a very powerful way to build and operate a better business, but there is also clear value to cease operating obsolete and inefficient systems. It is a trait of leadership to exercise courage to *stop* or say *no* to any practices and technologies that are well past their use-by date.

Finally, to get started on the technology journey, the ideal starting place is to know what the landscape looks like—determine the benefits to the business, understand the gaps from present performance, decide where to take the business over a one, two and three-year timeframe—and develop a roadmap to get there.

CHAPTER 17
Projects

From time to time, procurement is requested to support or lead business-wide or organisational directives and projects which relate to the role, but may be outside the mainstream activity of sourcing, contract management, supply chain assurance and other true core aspects of procurement's work. As they are projects, they are "one-off" in nature and have a defined life.

They include for example:

- Business transformation and cost reduction—This may arise if a business is in financial or trading difficulties and would include managing the impact of say a COVID-19 scenario

- Inventory reduction—This includes a project plan to achieve reduction and measures that sustain good inventory management practices.

There may be many more. It is quite natural for procurement to be selected for this work as there may well be a need to engage the supply community to assist in the project solution or involve processes that procurement is familiar with such as sourcing and negotiation.

At various stages in my working career I have been engaged in these types of projects, so I would like to share the ingredients of success as well as important learnings.

As noted throughout this book, for procurement to be held accountable for delivery of significant commercial value and function as a high-performing team—particularly in support of a major business turnaround, in response to the current global coronavirus pandemic and any other high-profile corporate-wide project work—a different operating model from traditional structures is required. The principal reasons for this include the urgency, the extent of project activity to prosecute, the quantum of value and risk involved and above all, the speed of decision-making required to close out supporting commercial deals and/or meet project deliverables.

This context is in fact the first learning outcome—recognising the difference in the nature of project work compared to mainstream procurement activity. Project timelines require urgency in delivery and the need to design and operate processes that are different to those standard authorised ones used to achieve required outcomes. For example, following the standard processes of a typical source program that may have a cycle time of two months when timelines require a turnaround of a week requires something different. In that instance, contract renegotiation may be more appropriate without any market engagement. Either that or following a source program that can be concluded in one week.

The second lesson is to recognise that procurement does not have authority within the confines of its role to prosecute large-scale, corporate-wide projects—they require the authority and sponsorship of the CEO/EXCO level, given these projects can extend to many facets of the business. This may sound obvious, but it is particularly relevant in the case of, say, inventory reduction. Procurement can always work in a continuous improvement mode and work within its authority to initiate small-step changes but that is as far as it can go. If a large-step change is required, then it becomes a business priority as other groups within the organisation will be impacted. Then, all senior leadership share in the same improvement equally to ensure any required changes are implemented. Also, the project structure and where procurement fits within it, needs to respect that any recommendations, general communications and change management required to deliver a project solution need to be reported in a format commensurate with the work of the CEO/EXCO role, given that is where sponsorship is likely to reside.

The third learning is to put the best people onto the work—it is not only a high-profile activity, but the work can be demanding. Only those who have developed skills in communication, who value the work and have a clear understanding of the need to have developed solutions consistent with required outcomes of the project should be given that responsibility.

Fourthly, a disciplined project management approach is required—discrete activities should be identified that make up the requirements of project deliverables, they should be resourced accordingly, deadlines noted, and activity value identified that cumulatively makes up the whole. The plan should be approved by the project sponsor and/or an EXCO or PSC.

And lastly, to keep focus on the work and maintain this as a business and team priority, reporting should be weekly and this cadence should continue until such time as the crisis has abated, business turnaround is complete or the project is significantly advanced.

Business Transformation and Cost Reduction

In projects such as these, particularly as business survival may depend on it, the entire spend base should be reviewed, placing priority on large-spend items, single-source supply chains and other items critical to business continuity. Here, the most likely and most immediate source of value would be to open contracts and renegotiate them to a level the business can afford. A standard script would be developed as shown in Chapter 6 (Sourcing). In addition, should a competitive market engagement process be necessary, then as also highlighted in that chapter, a one-page RFP should be deployed, stating business context and with a supporting CAC outlining a business requirement of 30 to 40 per cent reduction in cost measured on a TCI basis will be necessary to secure award. A one-week timeframe should be allowed for both contract renegotiations and sourcing programs that demonstrate the urgency of the work.

Again, it is essential that all work necessary to meet program outcomes should be converted into projects noting the project leader, expected completion date and project values that, cumulatively, meet the outcomes required from a target value perspective.

A similar project structure for supply chain assurance work (e.g., COVID-19) would be used, listing all major supply contracts that require renegotiation or resetting of commercial terms.

Inventory Reduction

My experience in this field is more concentrated in the resources and heavy engineering-type industries—but the principles of what I have written below would be valid for other business sectors as well.

There can be many contributing factors that require the need to examine inventory practices deployed leading to reduction through overinvestment. Often, the root of the issue lies in the fact inventory management and control does not carry the necessary level of importance and priority commensurate with its value. As a result, it tends not to have requisite capability applied to managing it. In addition, the role of the inventory controller may be poorly defined in terms of accountabilities and authorities and as a result, wrong measures are used for control of the asset.

A typical and common measure when considering inventory is to focus on its absolute value in monetary terms rather than its physical profile and whether that is requisite for the business. Maintenance teams have little appetite or incentive to reduce levels as they are driven by product availability and overinvestment results and with it a high level of slow-moving or obsolete stock. This disconnect between accountability and authority over inventory is the primary driver of overinvestment.

Of course, I am not inferring that all businesses exhibit overinvestment in inventory, nor am I saying there is a lack of capability applied. Merely, if its reduction has become a priority, then typical causes of overinvestment are often what I have described. I share these insights simply because past project plans to reduce inventory have failed to deliver results on a sustained basis. Nearly always, inventory levels did reduce after a level of management attention but slowly creeped up because the primary indicator was a lagging one, namely absolute inventory value and no regard was given for measures or changed practices as described in more detail below.

Taking all that into account, the starting point is to consider what the elements that make up *excellence* in inventory management are. Any gaps can give rise to the root cause of inventory inaccuracies and overinvestment. Below are seven key aspects that should be present:

- A warehouse to 5S standard (5S refers to sort, set in order, shine, standardise and sustain)—The warehouse needs to be clean, well lit, inventory tidy and supported by accurate record keeping, and location of items known. This will facilitate perpetual or annual stock counts

- Excellence in supplier management—Including supply chain management, DIFOT measured that is with lead times known/predictable, the business can manage their requisite holdings appropriately and avoid overinvestment. Suppliers should be deselected if poor performance contributes to lack of business continuity or delays in essential plant maintenance

- Inventory control—Recording system, reporting, accuracy, trend identification, leading indicators of build-up of investment and countermeasures deployed. The inventory controller requires the requisite authority to effectively manage the asset, namely to monitor and publish the key End of Line measure of *inventory turnover*, its trends over time, split between fast and slow-moving stock, suggested response plans for slow-moving stock, and accountability assignment to correct

- Accountability and ownership—These are an important aspect as quite typically a warehouse is managed by procurement and they have an accountability to ensure required items are available to meet plant demands; thus, they are held to account to provide a service to an operating site. Maintenance teams have no or little incentive to change anything (including lowering reorder levels, reacting to slow-moving items) and this is a source of major disconnect. Further, any inventory write-off would be to negatively impact the profit and loss account, thereby impacting cost targets and potentially the bonus calculations of the business. Thus, the incompatibility between accountability and authority between service provider and customer is apparent, resulting in an overinvestment as one group wants a low inventory level, and the other a high level to avoid the risk of compromising production. The desired outcome is that there is no disconnect

- The capability of maintenance planners and integrating requirements/ future activity with a planned, stable environment—This requires forecasting the right requirements and not in overinvestment

- The conservatism of the site generally—Reorder levels set by historical levels unrelated to present circumstances, lack of enthusiasm to reduce levels "just in case". Reorder levels need to be revisited frequently

- Use/non-use of supplier inventory ownership practices (Vendor Managed Inventory [VMI], consignment) etc., especially for high-value, insurance and long lead time items). Note that 3rd Party Logistics (3PL) businesses can take over a site's entire inventory, guarantee delivery of items to site within a defined timeframe and can potentially take the entire asset off the balance sheet, transferring immediate cash to site.

Once reorder levels are better defined/reduced and we know what is in the warehouse, we can then stop or reduce buying for overstocked, slow-moving items and utilise what we have before we go out and buy more—that action generates cash as we do not refill shelves, inventory goes down and turnover goes up. To get there you need to be *in control* and to get there and remain so, requires the requisite level of capability applied.

Project Plan to Reduce Inventory

Creating a project plan is a very big task—if the work is not done right and the requisite new practices are not put in place, inventory levels will quickly rise as the key controls will be absent. Potential scope of such a project activity will include the following steps:

- Develop a baseline and determine the gap to "best practice"—consider all inventories, practices, warehouses, safety performance, software deployed, metrics used, integration with maintenance/operations, levels of investment, inventory turnover, quality of leadership, and supplier performance

- From gap to best practice identified above, determine what is possible, what opportunities exist, how much inventory can be realised within six months, twelve months, or two years. Determine the level of conservatism in setting reorder levels and amend accordingly

- Re-present inventories into appropriate classifications (e.g., raw materials, consumables, fast-moving, slow-moving, obsolete, items held greater than nine months/two years, etc.)

- Identify immediate opportunities including "just do its"

- Consider alternate inventory holding strategies

- Develop pathway/project plan to realise goals, tasks, KPIs, reporting, tracking, leadership and resources required and changes required. Identify first things to do, second order, milestones and project governance

- Develop how to sustain and improve on benefits—new ways of working.

In many organisations, the warehouse is not considered one of the more interesting places to work, nor is it recognised by leadership as an area that requires significant attention or priority. Highlighting key measures such as inventory turnover, comparison to best practice and levels of overinvestment in such areas as slow-moving stock, usually succeeds in keeping management's attention and interest over this asset.

Measures and Practices—Inbound Supply Chain and Warehousing

To close the discussion on inventory management, below is a document that summarises those typical practices employed in warehouse inventory and compares those with a suggested new approach to managing this critical asset.

Supply Chain Excellence

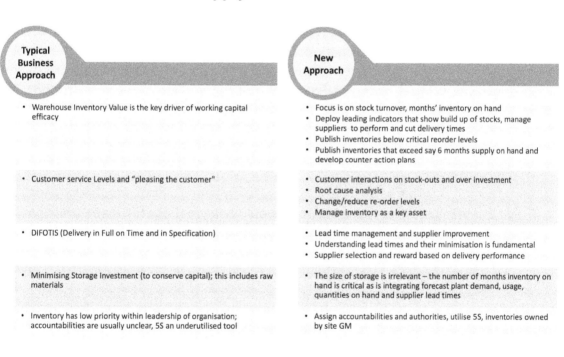

Typical Business Approach

- Warehouse Inventory Value is the key driver of working capital efficacy

- Customer service Levels and "pleasing the customer"

- DIFOTIS (Delivery in Full on Time and in Specification)

- Minimising Storage Investment (to conserve capital); this includes raw materials

- Inventory has low priority within leadership of organisation; accountabilities are usually unclear, 5S an underutilised tool

New Approach

- Focus is on stock turnover, months' inventory on hand
- Deploy leading indicators that show build up of stocks, manage suppliers to perform and cut delivery times
- Publish inventories below critical reorder levels
- Publish inventories that exceed say 6 months supply on hand and develop counter action plans

- Customer interactions on stock-outs and over investment
- Root cause analysis
- Change/reduce re-order levels
- Manage inventory as a key asset

- Lead time management and supplier improvement
- Understanding lead times and their minimisation is fundamental
- Supplier selection and reward based on delivery performance

- The size of storage is irrelevant – the number of months inventory on hand is critical as is integrating forecast plant demand, usage, quantities on hand and supplier lead times

- Assign accountabilities and authorities, utilise 5S, inventories owned by site GM

The right-hand column in the above diagram summarise what has been said above and shows that inventory management is an area that requires a capable leader including a number of defined role-vested authorities to succeed.

CHAPTER 18
Conclusion

My career in the procurement field has generated a lot of job satisfaction and I hope that is the same for you, the reader. My wish is that the level of satisfaction in procurement will rise if one or a few of the thoughts and ideas I have shared in this book can be applied to raise the perception of procurement in business and support career growth generally for practitioners. With technology advances, the work of procurement is becoming a lot more interesting and it is a key enabler to underpin transformation in the discipline.

Over the years, I have witnessed a number of tier one and tier two consulting firms support businesses to raise the level of procurement and extract more value from this essential function. Elevation of procurement can improve bottom line performance, reduce working capital, or influence other key metrics of businesses.

There are many reasons why a business would engage these firms and principal amongst them from a procurement perspective would be:

- Perception of a lack of skill level in procurement by senior leaders and therefore the potential exists to realise significant value for the business

- A lack of perceived leadership over the function by senior leaders

- There is a business crisis and large and immediate bottom line or cash flow improvement is required. The existing procurement team may not be up to the task

- Senior leadership require a peer review to verify the how the team performs relative to a benchmark.

There may, of course, be many more reasons.

The challenge that I will put forward is that some things never change. What I write below was as true 25 years ago as it is now, namely:

- The value that procurement can bring to an organisation is enormous

- The procurement team should be resourced with capable people

- The team should be led by a suitably skilled and capable practitioner who can demonstrate the key traits of leadership articulated in Chapter 1 (Getting the Fundamentals Right)

- Procurement requires visibility with senior leadership of the organisation

- The team needs to demonstrate they are professional in their work, disciplined in their approach, can work to a plan with a level of urgency and track and report their performance

- Procurement should select KPIs that are relevant to the leaders in the business so they can see the real value add of the team.

If all these elements were in place, there would be no or minimal need to engage outside procurement consultants, and indeed, that is largely what this book is all about.

It may sound trite to say this, but the main reason consultants earn a living from providing this service is exactly due to the reasons noted above, namely, there are gaps in procurement's performance. The preference, therefore, is to bring the expertise in-house and not have third parties run the business. I am not against the use of consultants, but my preference is to engage them for targeted and niche work, perhaps to provide some capacity to the team, but have the core and requisite skills stay in the business. After all, it is not always possible to keep up to date with latest thinking or leading practices, and engaging a third party to set a new horizon in performance is a way to lift both procurement's and the whole business's performance. Accordingly, one possible use of engaging a consulting firm is to support what is essentially proposed in this book, namely, establishing a PSC and all the change management processes that go with it to embed the new way of working.

The other aspect I have seen is the rush to adopt a new perceived best practice which provides the feeling of satisfaction that the business is doing the right thing. For example, an external party may write about or extol the benefits of *category management* or *e-auctions*. I am not about to dispel any good practice or idea; my caution is that implementing the latest idea may be only short-lived until replaced by another one. In fact, on that very point, engrained approaches, such as *global category management* which for many years have been the benchmark of success, are now being reconsidered. Specifically, what is required are far more adaptive and dynamic spend strategies that have a forward looking focus utilising predictive analytics which support differentiation, generate business and investment opportunities, have tighter integration with business performance metrics, are more flexible and responsive to emerging risks and opportunities.

Regardless of the merits of new ideas, the important factor is to never forget the drivers and elements of what makes a high-performing procurement team: leadership, reporting what is important to members of the PSC (viz. key business metrics), resourcing the team with capable personnel and possessing the agility to respond to challenges when they arise.

Referring to what I have written in Chapter 1 (Getting the Fundamentals Right), leadership is critical to the perception of procurement at an executive level and has been an issue for a number of years. It is why I have referred to it several times in this book. A study in 2019 reported by the tier one consulting firm, McKinsey, found that many executives see procurement as *purely a transactional function that executes commands and delivers goods*. Another study by Deloitte in 2018 reported that only 31 per cent of 504 respondents felt they were *highly supported* by their procurement function. It is therefore not surprising there are many external consultants supporting organisations and lifting procurement's performance.

For many successful procurement executives, leading the function and aligning procurement strategies to corporate objectives has ensured they have had a seat at the table. As I write this book during the current global crisis of COVID-19, it has placed this role and its teams in the spotlight like never before. It is for these reasons I strongly promote the establishment of a PSC that provides the authority for procurement to execute plans and strategies as well as an oversight body that provides essential support for the CPO's role.

In fact, COVID-19 has elevated procurement's involvement and importance within businesses as the need for security of supply is paramount, so now is the perfect opportunity for CPOs to step up and lead. Once the threat of COVID-19 passes, another business-critical issue or challenge will come along, so the occasion will always be present. Even if it is not, experience has shown that opportunities on some scale will always arise that can demonstrate the strategic potential and value that procurement provides.

Also, what I have written in this book is scalable. The key design elements should be apparent for a high-performing procurement team, but in small businesses, having direct access to the CEO may be sufficient without the need of a PSC. In that case, a monthly meeting with the same suggested PSC agenda may suffice. It will still require a good leader with capable support. Staffing levels will be less in small enterprises, so achieving the lofty heights of leading practice may be a stretch too far (or costly). I would still contend though that simple one-page tenders and RFP documents should be the norm, as described in Chapter 6 (Sourcing), with well-constructed CACs operating to tight cycle times to ensure rapid closure. These protocols, given their shortness and relative simplicity as market tools, will align well with operating a small business.

Before I sign off, a brief comment for you who may feel somewhat daunted or challenged by changing the organisational model to raise procurement's profile. If procurement is in the third or fourth tier of the business structure, or the value proposition of procurement is not resonating with senior leadership, there is a pathway forward. To overcome this, the following pointers can be considered:

- Carry out research on where procurement excellence can be demonstrated and speak to your line manager with an approach along the lines of, *"This is what we should do, how, when and here is the impact to us"* and give examples where value is being constrained in the business. If the manager says *NO*, seek advice from your manager once removed on how best to proceed—but that much depends on the relationship you have with that person. Of course, the reasons why the line manager says *NO* are an important lead into why procurement does not have the desired profile and the answer provided may result in developing the best solution to build the case for change

- Publish an article on LinkedIn or other platforms to advance your profile and seek peer support for ideas; consider those that have been proven to work

- Develop a one-page pro forma PSC report (refer to Chapter 4 on Procurement Steering Committee) as it would be applied to your business and demonstrate what the impact could be—or demonstrate the lost value potential—to senior leadership. Much of what is reported there, as well as the report design, will resonate well with that group, given its business impact.

The key before embarking on this course of action is to overcome the fear of leading. Communication upwards to promote change must be direct, data-driven, powerful and exude confidence. It must exhibit clarity on how to implement the new direction, what support is required and what will be done to assure success. The rewards will be worthwhile as once the keys to the door are provided to procurement, the potential is enormous.

If you were to ask me what the single, most important piece of advice I could offer all aspiring CPOs, what would it be? Naturally, this book contains many thoughts and ideas from my experience, they are all important, but it would be this. In a word, *communication* and to get into the habit of framing communication to senior levels in the business as though you were writing to the CEO of the business. Thus, short, clear, to the point and written in a style of "this is what it means to the business, its financial (or whatever) impact and this is the decision(s) required". Impactful business communication gets attention and when you talk the language of the business to senior leadership, they do become interested and you will get noticed. It takes work, thought and care; the results and benefits will come. Above all, communication develops a skill base beyond procurement as it speaks to understanding the business and the impact you are making.

If I reflect and consider when or what provided the catalyst to change my thinking away from following traditional procurement approaches, it would be the following. Near the end of my working career, I was in a business transformation program challenged to deliver an outcome of truly significant savings quickly, traceable to the bottom line. Part of the task was substantial cash generation. Following time-tested conventional protocols would take too long, and tie up significant resources with no guarantee of success and no hard linkage of outcomes to the financial statements. The required result was achieved and done so principally by following the concepts outlined in Chapter 5 (Commercial Award Criteria), Chapter 6 (Sourcing) and Chapter 17 (Projects) with strong support from top-line business leadership. After that, I never looked back as it was clear to me what I had done and have now shared with you in this book represents *good business*.

Just to emphasise the point further, after we were successful with the business turnaround, I provided a comment to the effect, "That was the best working experience of my life". It was not only the success of the project that drove the comment but also procurement's subsequent rise in both profile and status within the business. I saved the best for last and how often I reflect that if only I had applied earlier what I know now, what an incredible impact I could have made!

So, the journey ends with where the book begins—namely, to prioritise the appointment of a capable leader to establish and run the procurement function by doing the right work. What an opportunity it provides for those who can rise to the challenge, from the direct and visible contribution of bottom line performance to the impact on other key business metrics—and above all—the job satisfaction it generates for the leader and their team.

I wish you all well.

LIST OF ABBREVIATIONS

BATNA	Best Alternative for a Negotiated Agreement
BPO	Business Process Outsourcing
CAC	Commercial Award Criteria
CEO	Chief Executive Officer
CFO	Chief Financial Officer
COO	Chief Operations Officer
CPO	Chief Procurement Officer
CV	Curriculum Vitae
DIFOT	Delivery in Full and on Time
DIFOTIS	Delivery in Full, on Time and within Specification
EOI	Expression of Interest
ERP	Enterprise Resource Planning
EXCO	Executive Committee
GFC	Global Financial Crisis
HSE	Health, Safety and Environment
NPV	Net Present Value
PSC	Procurement Steering Committee
RFI	Request for Information
RFP	Request for Proposal
RFQ	Request for Quotation
TCI	Total Cost Impact
TCO	Total Cost of Ownership
VMI	Vendor Managed Inventory

Lightning Source UK Ltd.
Milton Keynes UK
UKHW030631050321
379837UK00010B/1572